THE
SCORPION
WITHIN

THE SCORPION WITHIN

REVEALING THE EIGHT DEMONIC ROOTS OF SIN

IRA MILLIGAN

© Copyright 2010—Ira Milligan

All rights reserved. This book is protected by the copyright laws of the United States of America. This book may not be copied or reprinted for commercial gain or profit. The use of short quotations or occasional page copying for personal or group study is permitted and encouraged. Permission will be granted upon request. Unless otherwise identified, Scripture quotations are taken from the King James Version. Scriptures identified as (NKJV) are taken from the New King James Version. Copyright © 1982 by Thomas Nelson, Inc. Used by permission. All rights reserved. Scriptures identified as (AMP) are taken from the Amplified® Bible, Copyright © 1954, 1958, 1962, 1964, 1965, 1987 by The Lockman Foundation. Used by permission. Emphasis within Scripture quotations is the author's own. Please note that Destiny Image's publishing style capitalizes certain pronouns in Scripture that refer to the Father, Son, and Holy Spirit, and may differ from some publishers' styles. Take note that the name satan and related names are not capitalized. We choose not to acknowledge him, even to the point of violating grammatical rules.

The graphic design for the Wheel of Nature is by Joseph Casey, Hermann, MO.

DESTINY IMAGE₈ PUBLISHERS, INC.

P.O. Box 310, Shippensburg, PA 17257-0310

"Speaking to the Purposes of God for This Generation and for the Generations to Come."

Previously published as *The Anatomy of a Scorpion* by Servant Ministries, Inc.

Previous ISBN: 0-9702375-1-0

This book and all other Destiny Image, Revival Press, MercyPlace, Fresh Bread, Destiny Image Fiction, and Treasure House books are available at Christian bookstores and distributors worldwide.

For a U.S. bookstore nearest you, call **1-800-722-6774**.

For more information on foreign distributors, call **717-532-3040**.

Reach us on the Internet: **www.destinyimage.com**.

Trade Paper ISBN-13: 978-0-7684-3236-7

Hardcover ISBN-13: 978-0-7684-3426-2

Large Print ISBN-13: 978-0-7684-3427-9

E-book ISBN-13: 978-0-7684-9061-9

For Worldwide Distribution, Printed in the U.S.A.

1 2 3 4 5 6 7 8 9 10 11 / 13 12 11 10

DEDICATION

This book is dedicated to my Mother, whom I dearly love. Her indomitable spirit, optimistic outlook, and plain hard work have been a constant inspiration to me throughout my life. Her often repeated admonition, "Where there's a will, there's a way," still rings in my ears when I meet direct opposition or encounter seemingly insurmountable difficulties. Words fail to describe the respect and admiration that I hold for her in my heart.

ACKNOWLEDGMENTS

I wish to express appreciation to my brother Alvin and my friends, Sally Miller and Jimmy Skinner, who freely gave of their time and efforts to read and critique this work. Their suggestions and corrections were immeasurably helpful.

TESTIMONY

The following letter from a man in California is typical of the many powerful testimonies that we receive from Christians who have read *The Scorpion Within*.

Dear Ira:

I attended one of your meetings in Placerville [California] a year or so ago, and my wife bought your books. I enjoyed the material then, but didn't really apply it earnestly to my life. My wife and her prayer partner are continually consulting the dreams book [referring to *Understanding the Dreams You Dream*]…it looks like a flower in bloom, it's been used so much. Anyway, a few weeks ago (in the Lord's timing) I opened the *Scorpion* book, applied it to myself, and went seriously after those principalities. I felt freedom for the first time in twenty years (I was born again 1976, ordained in 1980, and still in bondage in 1999…but no more!). Then last Friday we went to the Benny Hinn Crusade in Oakland, and I was filled to overflowing with the Holy Spirit. What a week!

I want to thank you again for the work you have done in the Lord Jesus, and for mailing me a copy of your new book….

In Christ Jesus,
W.S.

CONTENTS

PREFACE

This book is greatly condensed. Each chapter could easily be expanded into a complete book, and it would take just such an expansion to fully explain every precept that it introduces. Since time and space do not allow such expansion, I've included many Scripture references to aid the reader in further study.

This book introduces, logically and in order, the inner workings of God's most wonderful creation—*man*. Jeremiah's perplexing question, *"The heart is deceitful above all things, and desperately wicked: who can know it?"* (Jer. 17:9) reveals the complexity of His creation.

Complex, yes, but not beyond our ability to understand because as we study the Bible we find Jeremiah's question, *"Who can know it?"* is answered by John's testimony: *"Jesus...knew all men, and needed not that any should testify of man: for He knew what was in man"* (John 2:24-25). To this Paul adds, *"...We have the mind of Christ"* (1 Cor. 2:16). Consequently, if we have the mind of Christ, we, too, can comprehend what is in man's heart.

The Word of God is virtually a manufacturer's handbook of man, providing instructions for the maintenance and repair of God's handiwork. In it we have *"all things that pertain unto life and godliness"* (2 Pet. 1:3). Therefore, it is to this handbook, the Bible, that we must turn if we want to find the answers needed to understand ourselves. The explanations set forth in this volume come from the timeless wisdom of its pages.

There are many books already written on the nature of man. Some are written from a counselor's viewpoint, concerned with emotional healing. A few have been written on deliverance. This book brings additional knowledge into both of these areas of ministry.

In the past there has been more confusion surrounding emotional healing and deliverance than any other area of Christian doctrine. These truths have suffered greatly because of past excesses, ignorance, and abuse. Because of this, many churches have avoided these doctrines altogether; yet, no greater need exists in the Church today than proper counseling, inner healing, and deliverance.

In the Bible God declares: *"My people are destroyed for lack of knowledge"* (Hos. 4:6). It is my prayer that this book will aid in alleviating some of that lack. I pray that God will deliver many of His children from their captors through the knowledge provided herein. The brokenhearted children of God are healed by truth; truth alone can make them free. My hope is that many who have been blinded by the workers of darkness will receive their sight and liberty from their sins through this truth (see Luke 4:18).

I have written this book for the student and the teacher. For the student, it is written with a clear, concise, non-technical style, easy to comprehend. For the teacher, it is written in an orderly, logical manner with numerous Scripture references for systematic expansion and presentation of its contents. Using the references to both expound and expand the thoughts introduced in this book will provide much illumination to expose the evil workers of darkness and their unfruitful works.

May all who read and heed the instructions and admonitions set forth in this book give glory and thanks to God, through our Lord Jesus Christ, for every benefit they receive.

INTRODUCTION

Over 50 years have passed since I saw a scorpion for the first time. I was about 5 years old, lying in bed on a hot summer night. I glanced beside me and saw a small insect crawling toward me on the taut, white sheets.

This creature looked like a small, strange crawfish to me. Being from central Louisiana, like most boys from the Bayou State, I was quite familiar with crawfish.

Puzzled by the obvious differences between this creature and the more familiar crawfish, I called out to my mother: *"Come look at this little crawfish in my bed!"* Responding with both curiosity and alarm, my mother was even more alarmed at the sight of the menacing scorpion slowly crawling toward me.

Few insects have the power to invoke fear in us the way scorpions and spiders do. Fearing and detesting them, we endeavor to rid our lives of them as far as possible. In doing so, we reveal the divine abhorrence toward demons and sin that God formed in our spirits when we were created.

Although students of the Bible have long seen serpents as symbolic of demons, few realize the Scriptures also speak of scorpions and spiders as symbols of evil. The purpose of this book is to explain this symbolism and reveal how we may rid ourselves of the demons and sin that these creatures represent.

Chapter 1

THE SCORPION WITHIN

Behold, I give unto you power to tread on **serpents and scorpions***, and over all the power of the enemy: and nothing shall by any means hurt you...I thank Thee, O Father, Lord of heaven and earth, that Thou hast hid these things from the wise and prudent, and hast revealed them unto babes...* (Luke 10:19,21).

In this Scripture, Jesus gave His disciples complete authority and power over their enemies, but who are their enemies? The book of Revelation identifies one of the two creatures that Jesus spoke of, the serpent, as a symbol for the devil (see Rev. 12:9). Most Bible students are aware of this, but who, or what, does the scorpion represent? What authority and power lays hidden in the symbolism Jesus used concerning this creature?

Christians have overlooked, or perhaps disregarded, the fact that the Bible refers to both scorpions and serpents, and not serpents only. Paul was referring to the symbol of the scorpion when he wrote, *"O death, where is thy sting...the sting of death is sin; and the strength of sin is the law"* (1 Cor. 15:55-56).

As with most symbols used in Scripture, before one can understand this symbol's meaning, one must first understand the object which is used as a symbol, in this case, the scorpion. Scorpions belong to the same family of insects as spiders, and like spiders, have eight eyes and eight legs.[1] Scorpions also suck the body fluids of their prey like spiders. Unlike spiders, however, scorpions have two pincers which are used to hold their prey. Also, they kill their victims by a powerful stinger in their tails instead of by biting them. In some species their sting can even cause death in humans. Children are especially vulnerable.

As we carefully examine the Scriptures we'll see that *a scorpion represents the sin nature of our flesh and carnal mind*. The Bible also reveals that the nature of sin in man is the same as satan's character. The devil has four primary natures. They are *temptation, deception, accusation*, and *destruction* (see 1 Thes. 3:5; Rev. 12:9-11; 1 Cor. 10:10). These are inherent in the scorpion also (see James 1:14; Jer. 17:9; Rom. 2:14-15; Rev. 11:18).

The scorpion's right *pincer* represents *temptation*; the left *deception*. The *mouth* devours through *accusation* (see Gal. 5:15), and his *stinger* does the work of the *destroyer*. Satan takes full advantage of the scorpion's nature in men. Without it, he would not be able to persuade them to perform his evil deeds.

So we see that God, through this symbol, has revealed something to us about humanity in each part, or member, of the scorpion. *The eight eyes of the scorpion correspond to eight desires of the flesh and of the carnal mind.* These desires are common to all mankind because all humans are of like passion (see Prov. 23:5; Eph. 2:2-3; Acts 14:15).

The scorpion's legs represent eight roots of sin. These roots are the same as one's attitudes. God said it is at this level that man must overcome sin (see Luke 3:8-9). To sever a scorpion's legs is to render it powerless to fulfill its wicked desires.

Humanity's natural tendency to sin is comparable to satan's corrupt nature, so when people overcome and crucifies their sinful disposition, they get victory over satan (see 1 John 3:8). Jesus said, "...*The prince of this world cometh, and hath nothing* [no sinful disposition] *in Me*" (John 14:30).

The devil was powerless over Jesus because He had crucified the sinful desires of His flesh (see Luke 4:1-13; Heb. 4:15). There was no likeness of satan in Christ. Likewise, it is only when people place their carnal lusts on the cross that they are liberated from the power of sin (see Rom. 6:11-14).

Endnote

1. The number of eyes varies in different species.

Chapter 2

SIN'S AGENT

He that committeth sin is of the devil; for the devil sinneth from the beginning. For this purpose the Son of God was manifested, that He might destroy the works of the devil (1 John 3:8).

Sin's primary agent is satan, *"the spirit that now worketh in the children of disobedience..."* (Eph. 2:2, see also John 8:44). There would be very little mischief in the world today if it were not for sin's super salesman. Although James said that men are drawn into sin through their own lust, the one enticing them to err is the devil (see James 1:13-15). Eve was not disobedient until the serpent prompted her to emulate God (see Gen. 3:1-6). Likewise, the Scriptures record that satan tempted David to number Israel, convincing him to sin through pride (see 1 Chron. 21:1). He also put an evil scheme into Judas' heart and persuaded him to betray Jesus. After Judas acted upon his suggestion, satan entered into him to motivate him to carry out his treachery (see John 13:2,27).

Demons are active in almost all sin. As a result, a proper understanding of satan and his demons is essential if we are to overcome our natural tendency to transgress God's commandments (see 1 John 3:4,8,10; Eph. 6:11-12; Matt. 4:1; John 8:44; Acts 13:8-10; 1 Cor. 7:5; James 4:7).

Jesus acknowledged that satan was the chief of all demons (see Luke 11:15-19). Revelation 12:9 adds "devil" as a proper name for satan and confirms that the serpent which deceived Eve in the Garden of Eden was satan. Jesus called him, *"the prince of this world"* (John 12:31), and Paul used the phrase, *"the prince of the power of the air"* in reference to him

(Eph. 2:2). Paul also called him, *"the god of this world"* (2 Cor. 4:4). All three phrases indicate that satan has superiority among evil spirits.

Because satan is the prince of demons, it is obvious that he governs the unclean spirits who live in and influence people. Although some Christians question whether the devil, as an individual, can live inside a person, the Bible specifically states that he can. There are two Scriptural examples of satan actually being inside people. John said satan entered into Judas before he betrayed Christ (see John 13:27), and Peter asked Ananias why he had allowed satan to fill his heart to lie to the Holy Ghost (see Acts 5:3).

In addition to satan working *in* and *through* people, God's Word reveals that he works evil *upon* people, too. Jesus loosed (delivered) a woman from a *"spirit of infirmity."* Afterward, He said that satan had bound her (see Luke 13:11-16). Likewise, when Job was smitten with his infirmity of boils, satan deserved and received the blame (see Job 2:7).

When we examine the kingdom of darkness, we discover a very systematic, well-organized system in operation. Jesus taught that demons cooperate among themselves, and even help one another if someone casts out one of them. By mutual support and teamwork, demons strive to reenter a person after they are thrown out. They work together to repossess everything they have lost. Contrary to common belief, demons do not fight among themselves. Jesus said that if satan divided his own kingdom, it would not stand (see Luke 11:17-26).

From this, one can conclude that satan skillfully commands and directs his demonic forces. Although it appears that he seldom dwells in humans personally, he is responsible for those who do. Because he has authority over all other evil spirits, he is responsible for their actions. Therefore, he deserves the blame for most of the sin and sickness that is in the earth (see Matt. 9:32-33, 12:22, 15:22; John 8:44; Acts 10:38; 1 Cor. 7:5; 1 John 3:8).

Chapter 3

THE LAW OF DOMINION

*Shall the throne of iniquity have fellowship with thee, which frameth mischief by **a law?** (Psalm 94:20)*

The Bible teaches that satan uses God's Law to work his evil in the earth (see Rom. 7:10-11; 1 Cor. 15:55-56). The specific law spoken of here in Psalm 94:20 is the *Law of Dominion.* Paul said:

Know ye not, that to whom ye yield yourselves servants to obey, his servants ye are to whom ye obey; whether of sin unto death, or of obedience unto righteousness? (Romans 6:16)

Jesus' terse statement in John 8:34 is even clearer: *"Whosoever committeth sin is the servant of sin."* The meaning of this is simple. Once a person yields to temptation and sins, satan gains authority to compel that person to continue violating God's will. But, even so, those who claim, "The devil made me do it" usually must admit they first chose to yield their members to sin before it became compulsory.

For instance, before Judas actually betrayed Jesus, the devil first tempted him with the idea. Satan submitted the evil plan to him long before he ate the choice morsel Jesus offered him at their last supper together (see Prov. 21:27; John 13:2). Until then, it was only a thought—an evil imagination. But when Judas pretended to be Jesus' friend by accepting His gift and eating with Him, he lied by his actions. By lying, he submitted to the tempter and yielded himself to sin. Then satan entered into him and motivated him to carry out his devilish plan (see Matt. 27:18; John 12:4-6,

13:26-27). By giving in to his own greed and envy, Judas became an instrument for satan to use to work mischief against our Lord.

Yielding to iniquity constitutes a covenant. Amos 3:3 states, *"Can two walk together except they be agreed?"* An agreement is the same as a covenant or contract. It should be regarded the same as a vow. A covenant can be entered into by word or deed and, like a vow, is perpetually binding until it is annulled, fulfilled, or forgiven (see Gen. 9:16, 17:7; Num. 6:2,5, 30:2-15; Deut. 23:21; 1 Sam. 18:3; 2 Sam. 9:1,6-7; Eccl. 5:4-5; Isa. 55:3; Heb. 13:20).

An example of how an evil covenant has a lasting and detrimental effect upon one's life can be seen in the record of Joshua being deceived by the people of Gibeon. God gave Joshua strict orders not to make any covenant with the people of Canaan (see Deut. 7:2). But, some of the elders of Gibeon tricked Joshua into thinking they were from a far-off nation. He thought these men were potential friends, but actually they were his enemies. Because he was deceived, he broke God's commandment and made a treaty with them. Three days later he discovered his mistake.

Although the Gibeonites misled Joshua when he entered into covenant with them, both he and the people of Israel were obligated to keep it. Since Joshua was the head of the nation, all Israel was bound by the terms of his agreement (see Josh. 9:13-19).

Several hundred years later, in his zeal for Israel, King Saul broke Joshua's covenant with the Gibeonites. Later Saul died on the battlefield, and David was made king. But as a result of Saul's sin of covenant breaking, a famine came upon the nation. Although it was hundreds of years after Joshua had made the covenant, it was still in force. Even though the man who sinned and broke the covenant was dead, his sin was very much alive. Once judgment came and the curse was applied, Israel did not receive any more rain until they made an atonement for Saul's sin (see 2 Sam. 21:1-10; Eccl. 5:4-6).

David was perplexed because he could not understand why his nation was undergoing a famine. He did not perceive there was a connection between the peoples' starvation and the ancient covenant broken by King Saul. Isaiah warned Israel (and all who have ears to hear) of the destructive and lasting effects of an evil covenant:

> *Because ye have said, we have a covenant with death, and with hell are we at agreement; when the overflowing scourge shall pass through, it shall not come unto us; for we have made lies our refuge, and under falsehood have we hid ourselves; Therefore thus saith the Lord…"Your covenant with death shall be disannulled, and your agreement with hell shall not stand; when the overflowing scourge shall pass through, then* **ye shall be trodden down by it***. From the time that it goes forth it shall take you: for morning by morning shall it pass over, by day and by night; and it shall be a vexation only to understand the report* (Isaiah 28:15-19).

Being trodden down is depression. People may be depressed mentally, emotionally, socially, financially, or even physically (by sickness). Regardless of the type of depression, it is often the product of an evil covenant made through sin. Proverbs 26:2 states, *"…The curse causeless shall not come."*

Nearly all of the Law's curses can be summed up into two components—*slightness of provision* (including the loss of one's health) and *loss of honor* (see Prov. 5:9-10, 6:26,33; James 4:4). Concerning the first component, the loss of provision, whether the provision is necessary to meet an essential need or simply to satisfy a desire, a curse limits the available supply, causing a shortage.

Second, the loss of honor may be a demotion or the loss of a promotion. Either way, it is often the work of a curse. Also, a disgrace brought upon one through the shameful actions of a family member is typical of such a curse. An evil slander spoken by an envious *"friend"* is another example (see Prov. 26:28).

Christians are delivered from the curse of the Law through the cross of Christ. There is no curse upon those who have fully repented and are covered by the blood of Jesus. But if one yields his members to sin after being saved he renews his old covenant of sin and becomes a servant of sin. Then, because of his transgression, the cross of Christ becomes of no affect and the curse is revived (see Gal. 3:13; Rom. 6:16).

In addition to this, until people are enlightened by God's Word (or Spirit) as to what actually constitutes sin, they cannot fully repent. They cannot repent of something that they have not recognized as wrong. Nevertheless, until people repent, satan takes advantage of their ignorance and administers the curse. God said, *"My people are destroyed for lack of knowledge..."* (Hos. 4:6; see also Num. 15:27-28).

The Deceitfulness of Sin

Once people have been enlightened, it is easy for them to see that such things as playing with Ouija boards, going to fortune tellers, and partaking of séances are all agreements (or covenants) with satan. If they were partakers of such, by yielding themselves and their members to iniquity, they became a servant of those spirits that enticed and enchanted them (see Deut. 18:9-12).

But the covenants made through religious affiliations are not so obvious. When people join religious organizations, they make a covenant. Also, if children's parents are members of a religion when they are born, the children are born under a spiritual covenant, as Samson was (see Judges 13:3-5) This may be good, or it can be evil. It depends upon what the covenant consists of (see Neh. 9:38, 10:28-29; Phil. 3:5; 2 Tim. 1:5).

Many religious organizations of our day limit the power of God. For example, some theologians say that miracles were just for the early church. By denying that God's miracle power is available to the Church today, they grieve Him. God is supernatural. Without faith in His power, it is impossible to please Him (see Ps. 78:40-41; Heb. 11:6; 2 Tim. 3:5).

Likewise, several of the religious organizations in existence today believe and teach that God no longer gives the Holy Spirit to believers. By rejecting the baptism of the Holy Spirit, they also reject the power to heal the sick and cast out devils that accompanies the baptism (see Acts 1:8). Today, many Christians are like the Sadducees of Jesus' day; they do not know the Scriptures nor the power of God (see Matt. 22:29-32; 2 Tim. 4:2-4).

When an organization's doctrines limit God, forming boundaries or bondage in the lives of God's people, it restricts the operation of His power working in their lives (see Matt. 13:58; Mark 7:13). The spirits that work through the authority of government enforce those boundaries (see Acts 9:1-2; 1 Tim. 4:1).

Submitting to an organization that limits or misrepresents God constitutes a covenant agreement. People who have been a member of one or more of them, by birth or by choice, are under a covenant.

Once people discover that they are under a religious covenant that limits God, they usually repent of the error of their ways and change denominations or churches. But when they break the barriers that were made by the doctrines they previously submitted to, they break a covenant. Covenant breaking is sin. If they want to be free, they must do more than tear themselves away from past doctrinal errors. According to the Bible, they must break their ties and destroy their barriers by confessing and renouncing them as sin (see Eccl. 5:4-6; 2 Cor. 4:2, 11:3-4; 2 Tim. 3:5).

Christians must renounce, *"the hidden things of dishonesty"* (2 Cor. 4:2) including the doctrines of men and demons to which they have previously submitted. When people are in covenant agreement with an organization, because of the Law of Dominion, they are under the authority of the spirits that control that organization:

> *Know ye not, that to whom ye yield yourselves servants to obey,*
> *his servants ye are to whom ye obey...* (Romans 6:16).

When people confess their former covenants and agreements as sin, they put them under Christ's blood. Through obeying God and confessing and forsaking their sin, they sever the cords of iniquity by which they were bound (see Prov. 5:22, 28:13).

Involuntary Service

Another important aspect of the Law of Dominion is stated in Second Peter 2:19: *"...Of whom a man is overcome, of the same is he brought in bondage."* It is because of this aspect of the Law of Dominion that God commands His children not to provoke their own children to anger (see Eph. 6:4; Col. 3:21). A child punished harshly in anger is overcome by resentment. The resentment then opens the child's heart to receive a spirit of anger, and the evil cycle continues.

An abused child frequently becomes a child abuser. Sometimes abusers realize their sinful error, but are unable to change. They cannot correct their behavior by willpower alone. Often they want to do what is right, but simply do not have the ability to change (see Rom. 7:18-19).

The Law of Dominion has a profound influence upon everyone. For this reason, we need to examine one more feature of it. *It was the Law of Dominion that gave the devil authority over the earth when Adam sinned.* In the beginning, Adam received authority over everything God created (see Heb. 2:6-7). As a result, satan obtained this authority when he gained dominion over Adam. Adam was the head. *To control the head is to control the entire body.* This principle is true whether the control is obtained through voluntary submission or by conquest. This fundamental truth is revealed in Goliath's challenge to Israel:

> *And he stood and cried unto the armies of Israel, and said unto them... "Choose you a man for you, and let him come down to me. If he be able to fight with me, and to kill me, then will we be your servants: but if I prevail against him, and kill him, then shall ye be our servants, and serve us"* (1 Samuel 17:8-9).

When people defeat a principality (a ruling spirit of satan's forces), they gain authority over all the spirits that are subject to that principality. Likewise, when satan gains control over a person who is in authority, he gains dominion over all the people who are subject to that person's authority! This is the reason Paul warned his followers that a Christian's warfare is, *"against the rulers of darkness of this world, against spiritual wickedness in high places"* (Eph. 6:12).

These high places are natural positions of authority! The President; Supreme Court Justices; senators; legislators; state governors, and local authorities are all rulers in high places. When spiritual wickedness operates in kings, governors, mayors, popes, priests, pastors, and other such authorities, evil prevails in the midst of the population.

Many Christians think these high places are in the air over nations and cities. In contradiction to this Paul said, *"So fight I, **not** as one that beateth the air"* (1 Cor. 9:26). Spiritual warfare is with demons *in* people, not demons in the air. Although it is certain that some demons exist in the air, they are powerless to influence the affairs of men until they inhabit someone. For example, government officials influenced by men and women embittered against God by evil spirits make laws against prayer in schools and then enforce those laws.

Another example is that demons in men in high places of authority (not demons in the sky) cause those men and women to consent to the killing of unborn babies by abortion. Thousands of unborn babies die each day while the Church's intercessors shout, *"I bind you, satan."* They fight against the air while satan laughs at their ignorance.

When a ruler submits to evil, satan obtains the right to work that same evil among the people subject to that ruler's authority. That is the reason Paul charged everyone to pray for kings, and for all who are in authority (see 1 Tim. 1:18, 2:2-1). To be both efficient and effective in spiritual warfare, the Church's prayer warriors must *"fight only with the king"* (see 2 Chron. 18:30).

For example, the Bible reveals that much of the trouble Daniel faced came from the kings of Babylon and Persia. An angel visited Daniel and informed him that the answer to his prayer had been delayed because he had been fighting with the authority Daniel was under—demons, in the kings of Persia. The angel said, *"I remained there with the Kings of Persia"* (while the battle was being fought). The battle was fought in the souls of men in authority—then—and now (see Dan. 10:12-13).

> *The Kings of the earth stood up* [or, have taken their stand], *and the rulers were gathered together against the Lord, and against His Christ* [anointed] (Acts 4:26).

The Church is the anointed of God. God's Saints are the anointed ones whom the authorities are taking a stand against. God's people are being robbed by ignorance. The Church's prayer warriors must direct their arrows (prayers) at the proper target—those men and women, in authority, who are yielding themselves to demonic influence.

If the Church would have known how to fight, it would not have lost the liberty for America's children to pray in school. When the King of Persia forbade his subjects to pray, Daniel openly resisted the evil law. He won his battle by knowledgeable prayer. At the time of this writing, the Church still has not won that conflict. In this *"Christian"* nation, children are still forbidden to openly pray in school (see Dan. 6:7-13).

Ruling authorities, influenced by evil spirits, pass evil and burdensome laws and rules. Through the enforcement of these laws by lower authorities, satan forces his evil deeds upon the people. Once corrupt officials and leaders have introduced and established unrighteous laws and customs into a society, the Church must pray and resist these evil ways until the populace returns to God. To accomplish this, the Church must sincerely repent. Christians need to confess and renounce their own sins *and* those of their forefathers. Then they must bring forth works of righteousness in opposition to the evil ways their society has fallen into (see Lev. 26:39-42; Jon. 3:4-10; Luke 3:7-14).

The Law of Dominion clearly reveals the importance of having righteous men and women in government. Christians should pray for the exposure and eradication of spiritual wickedness and corruption in high places. Light destroys darkness. Deceitful and perverted senators, representatives, governors, mayors, police chiefs, and even pastors must be exposed.

All dishonesty and corruption of those holding responsible positions of government must be uncovered.

Ephesians 5:11 (AMP) commands us to expose, reprove, and convict the unfruitful works of darkness. Hidden wickedness cannot be reproved, but when deceitful works become public, the light of exposure defeats and destroys them. Darkness cannot exist in the presence of light. But Jesus warned that light (that which is esteemed as truth) can be darkness (see Matt. 6:23).

Once a society becomes obsessed with iniquity, immoral rulers can persist even after their wickedness is exposed. When a nation condones abortion, infidelity, divorce, pornography, fornication, sodomy, profanity, drunkenness, drugs, and such ungodliness, that nation has reached the fullness of iniquity. *When exposure of evil no longer brings a reproach upon evil doers, there is no repentance possible—the only alternative is destruction* (see Gen. 15:16, 19:9,13-15; Ps. 9:17; Rom. 1:32):

> *For the wrath of God is revealed from heaven against all ungodliness and unrighteousness of men, who hold the truth in unrighteousness* (Romans 1:18).

That is all the more reason why the Church should intercede for those officials and leaders who *do* know and serve the Lord Jesus. They should pray for them to be bold and take a strong stand for righteousness. Leaders ruling in righteousness are a blessing to their country. For this reason, satan fights all leaders to overthrow them with sin (see Prov. 29:2; 2 Thess. 3:1-2).

When Moses, the highest authority in Israel, was supported and his hands were lifted up by Aaron and Hur, Israel won their battle. When he was weak and there was no intercession, they lost (see Exod. 17:8-14). When Israel's kings were righteous, all Israel had revival. But when spiritual wickedness was in the high place of the king's office, sin prevailed over the nation (see 2 Chron. 29:1-10, 30:4-20, 31:1, 33:1-10,17).

The head, through the Law of Dominion, determines whether the people walk in righteousness or wickedness. The head has power to subdue the body. The body does whatever the head commands it to do if it is a healthy body. If the head is righteous, the body does righteousness. If the head is evil, the fruit of the body cannot be good (see Matt. 7:18):

> *While they promise them liberty, they themselves are the servants of corruption: for of whom a man is overcome* [or ruled by], *of the same is he brought in bondage* (2 Peter 2:19).

There are *12 Universal Laws of the Universe*. Of the 12, none has a more far-reaching effect upon people's lives than *The Law of Dominion*.[1]

Endnote

1. The 12 Universal Laws of the Universe are:

    1. **Praise and Worship** (see Ps. 16:11, 22:3, 50:23, 66:18; Matt. 6:21-24; Luke 11:41)

    2. **Hearing**—judging whether to accept or reject (thus obey or disobey) that which is heard (see Isa. 1:19-20; Luke 8:18; John 5:30)

    3. **Dominion**—voluntary and involuntary submission (Ps. 94:20; John 8:34-36; Rom. 6:16; 2 Pet. 2:19)

    4. **Stewardship**—responsibility and faithfulness (see Luke 12:48, 16:10-12, 19:13-27; 1 Cor. 4:2)

    5. **Promotion and Demotion** (see Ps. 75:6-7; Prov. 3:34-35, 18:12, 22:4; Matt. 23:12; Mark 9:35)

6. **Patience and Persistence**—importunity (see Luke 11:5-10, 18:1-8, 21:19; Heb. 6:12)

7. **Division and Unity** (see Gen. 11:1-8; Matt. 12:25, 18:18-20; James 1:6-8)

8. **Sowing and Reaping**—harvest (see Gen. 1:11-12; Prov. 24:11-12; Isa. 3:10-11; Matt. 7:1-2,17-18; Luke 6:38; 2 Cor. 9:6; Gal. 6:7-8)

9. **Sin and Death** (see Gen. 2:17; Ezek. 18:20; Rom. 7:21-23)

10. **Righteousness**—the Royal Law or the Law of Love (see Lev. 18:5; Deut. 6:25; Rom. 9:30-31, 10:4, 13:8-10; Gal. 5:14; James 2:8)

11. **Faith and Action**—works (see Matt. 9:29, 17:20; Mark 9:23, 11:23-24; Rom. 1:17, 3:27; James 2:20-24)

12. **The Spirit of Life and Liberty** (see John 8:35-36; Rom. 4:6-8, 8:1-4; Gal. 5:1,13; James 1:25, 2:12-13)

Chapter 4

EIGHT CATEGORIES OF SIN

*But the **fearful**, and **unbelieving**, and the **abominable** [despising], and **murderers**, and **whoremongers** [fornication], and **sorcerers**, and **idolaters**, and all **liars**, shall have their part in the lake which burneth with fire and brimstone; which is the second death* (Revelation 21:8).

All iniquity can be grouped into one or more of the eight categories of sin which are enumerated in Revelation 21:8. The importance of understanding these eight categories becomes evident when one considers what the Bible says about eradicating sin. The Scriptures state that to eliminate sin one must use an axe. Sin's root must be cut. John the Baptist said, *"The axe is laid unto the root of the trees..."* (Luke 3:9). Knowing the identity of each tree enables one to identify and locate its root. Because there are only eight trees, there are only eight roots to contend with.

Following are several examples of sin in each different category: When Joshua conquered Jericho, the spoils of war were supposed to be consecrated to God. But one of Joshua's men, Achan, coveted and stole some of the plunder. According to Colossians 3:5, Achan's act of covetousness and his sin of stealing were *idolatry* (see Josh. 6:18-19, 7:20-25).

Another example is the biblical story of Amnon, who raped his half-sister. Pretending to be sick, Amnon lured Tamar into being alone with him and forced her. After he had satisfied his lust, he thrust her away from him because of his hatred for women (see 2 Sam. 13:6-16; Deut. 22:25-26). One such as Amnon, a rapist, normally hates women (*murder*) and is filled with lust (*fornication*). Amnon also deceived her with his actions (*lying*).

King Saul gives us another example. Saul only partially performed the will of God when Samuel sent him to destroy the Amalekites. Samuel summed up Saul's failure and stubborn disobedience in two words—*sorcery* and *idolatry*. Careful study of this passage of scripture will also reveal the sin categories of *unbelief* and *fearfulness* (see 1 Sam. 15:2-3;17-30).

David's infamous affair with Bathsheba falls into the sin classification of whoremonger (*fornication*). Then his fearful and vain attempts to cover his sin come under *fearfulness* and *lying*. Finally, he committed a deceitful act of *murder* against Uriah, at the hands of the children of Ammon, and then took Uriah's wife as his own, thus *despising* God (see 2 Sam. 11:1-25, 12:9).

We will examine each of these examples in greater detail as we continue to uncover the sin nature of man.

Chapter 5

THE PARADOX OF NATURE

What is the sin nature? The Bible states that people are created in the image of God (see Gen. 1:27). If so, why are people so prone to sin? James said, "...*God cannot be tempted with evil, neither tempteth he any man*" (James 1:13). If people are made in His image, why then are they tempted continuously?

A Mirror

To answer this question one must understand several concepts about God's Word. First, the Bible teaches that *the Word of God is a mirror* (see 1 Cor. 13:12; James 1:23-25). *A mirror reverses the image revealed in it.* God's Word was made flesh; as a result, man's flesh is the mirror image, or reverse image, of God (see John 1:14).

God cannot lie. People, however, must constantly watch, in word and action, to keep from lying. God is never tempted with evil; however, because humanity's flesh is the exact copy of God, in reverse, people are tempted continuously. God hates sin; as a result, people are passionately drawn toward it. God is light; therefore, humanity's carnal nature is total darkness (see Eph. 5:8). Finally, God is love, but people are consumed with selfishness.

When Bible students look at the Word (the Mosaic Law) that became flesh, they do not behold a God of love. God is Love, but the Law reveals God as a strict, harsh, demanding, unapproachable Judge. The Law is a mirror; therefore, that which one sees in the Law is the antithesis, or reverse, of that which God actually is (see Exod. 19:10-24; Heb. 4:15-16, 12:18-21).

A Vessel

Another concept to help one understand this paradox is this: The Word made flesh is a *vessel*. Jesus was God's vessel. He said the flesh profits nothing (see John 6:63). It is only a container. *"God was in Christ, reconciling the world to Himself..."* (2 Cor. 5:19). Likewise, people are made as vessels unto honor, to reveal God's Spirit to the world (see Rom. 9:21-23; 2 Tim. 2:20-21). Paul said, *"We have this treasure in earthen vessels, that the excellency of the power may be of God, and not of us"* (2 Cor. 4:7).

When a vessel is filled with water, the liquid conforms to the contour of the vessel's interior. The shape of the receptacle is the opposite of the liquid it contains. Likewise, when a mold is made to produce a solid object, the mold is formed in the reverse likeness of the article it is designed to produce.

A vessel's interior is called the container's heart. Likewise, the inner portion of the vessel made for God is the heart. Humanity's heart was made as a receptacle for God. As a result, it is God's perfect likeness, only transposed. Like a mold to pour brass into, or ceramics, it is the reverse of the image it was created to produce (see 1 Kings 7:45-47; 1 Cor. 15:45-49).

Humanity's heart is designed to contain and reveal God's divine nature. Humanity's spirit was fashioned into the Creator's exact likeness (see Gen. 1:26-27); therefore, it perfectly fits within the vessel of clay God made for it.

Jesus was the Word made flesh. When He died on the cross, the container, or mold, was broken. This happened so the precious treasure it contained could be poured out upon all flesh (see John 16:7; Acts 2:17). Paul said:

> [We are] *Always bearing about in the body the dying of the Lord Jesus, that the life also of Jesus might be made manifest in our body. For we which live are always delivered unto death* [broken] *for Jesus' sake, that the life also of Jesus might be made manifest in our mortal flesh* (2 Corinthians 4:10-11).

> *We glory in tribulations also...because the love of God is shed abroad* [from the broken vessel] *in our hearts by the Holy Ghost which is given unto us* (Romans 5:3-5).

A House

In Acts 7:49, God asked: *"What house will ye build Me? ...What is the place of My rest?"* The Church, which is the Bride of Christ, was formed to be both *God's vessel and His house* (see Eph. 5:22-32; Heb. 3:6; 2 Tim. 2:20-21). God made the human body as a house for Himself (see 1 Cor. 3:9,16-17). The interior of this house, or vessel, is made in the reverse image of the One who desires to dwell in it. This is the reason the natural disposition of humanity's flesh is the opposite of God's Spirit.

The husband and wife relationship is another parable demonstrating this truth. When the bride truly submits to her husband, she takes on his nature, and his life becomes her life (see Gen. 2:23-24; 1 Cor. 11:3; Gal. 2:20). Often she must relinquish her will to be able to submit to her husband's. Likewise, *people become partakers of the divine nature of God through submission to Him.* When people are obedient to God, they escape the corruption that is in the world through the natural lust of their flesh (see Acts 5:32; 2 Pet. 1:4).

Eve was a living vessel. Satan took advantage of her innocence and used the nature of her flesh to lure her into disobedience. Her flesh's nature was the exact opposite of God's, so it was easy for him to use it against God (see Gen. 3:1-6; 1 Pet. 3:7).

From the beginning satan coveted God's house, or bride. He determined to oppose God (see Isa. 14:12-14). When satan chose to rebel against God to satisfy his evil ambition, he became forever bound to iniquity. Once the devil turned against God, he could not repent. He is, *"reserved in everlasting chains under darkness unto the judgment of the great day"* (Jude 6). Bound and doomed in eternal darkness, he is the enemy of all light (see Acts 13:10-11).

Satan, by his own decision, is the opposite of God. He cannot live in the vessel made for God, as God does. God joins His spirit to the spirit of mankind as a bride is joined to her husband. Then both live in the heart of flesh God has made for them (see Ezek. 36:26-27; 1 Cor. 6:17,19).

The human spirit is in the exact likeness of God's; *therefore, it is not compatible with the devil's spirit.* Satan and his demons are compatible only with the flesh. They live in the vessel itself, not inside the container, but *in the walls* of the vessel. In this way, satan's demons are able to use the life of the flesh to express themselves and fulfill their cravings.

Paul said, *"For I know that in me (that is, in my flesh,) dwelleth no good thing..."* (Rom. 7:18). He then went on to say that sin was in his members, plainly indicating that the dwelling place of demons is in man's flesh (see Rom. 7:17-18).

Much like termites live inside the walls of a house (to the destruction of the house), demons live in the flesh of humans (see Gen. 3:14). Likewise, as termites cannot tolerate light, because demons are darkness they are dispelled by light (see John 3:19-20; Eph. 5:8-13).

The Nature of Our Spirit

God created the human spirit as an accurate reproduction of His own. God breathed into Adam's body the breath of life, and by this He imparted unto Adam a living spirit.

It is for this reason, by the nature of their spirits, that people agree with God in their consciences. Jesus said people are ready and willing to obey and serve Him with their spirits, but their flesh is *"weak"* or unable (see Matt. 26:41; Mark 14:38; Rom. 1:9). In Romans 2:14, Paul said the Gentiles, *"do by* [their spirits'] *nature the things contained in the law...."*

Jesus referred to this natural tendency of the human spirit to concur with, and be like God, when He instructed His disciples to observe children as a model of humility and kindness (see Matt. 18:2-4). Children reveal the divine nature quite naturally before their hearts are hardened through the deceitfulness of sin (see Heb. 3:12-13).

This is the reason the Scripture teaches Christians to *renew* their minds; they do not have to obtain a new one (see Ps. 51:10; Rom. 12:2). *The natural mind one had as a child was a spiritual mind.* The carnal mind develops as one matures in age. Satan then works through the carnal mind, bringing the mind of the spirit into captivity.

Adults manifest the divine nature only when God dwells in them and governs the vessel, or house. When the carnal mind is mature, people cannot reveal the true treasure they were designed to disclose without God's help. People fall into sin because of the weakness of their flesh (see Ps. 51:5; Rom. 3:23; Heb. 3:6-12).

> *For from within, out of the heart of men* [adults], *proceed evil thoughts, adulteries, fornications, murders...blasphemy, pride, foolishness; All these evil things come from within, and defile the man* (Mark 7:21-23).

When a child is very young his innocent and naive heart is easily harmed and captured. God told Jeremiah to observe the making of a vessel by a potter to teach him the ease with which the enemy ruined His original handiwork. The potter easily formed the soft clay into a vessel, but the vessel was just as easily damaged because it was so pliable (see Jer. 18:1-4).

The devil works to mar the vessel created by and for God through self-justification. His aim is to corrupt the receptacle designed and fashioned for the revelation of God's goodness (see Eph. 2:10). *By twisting and warping the vessel (man's mind), the interior (heart) becomes distorted and will bring forth satan's likeness instead of God's.* Satan's evil purpose is to manifest his own foul nature through man instead of allowing God to reveal His divine nature (see John 8:44).

After satan's demons have warped and twisted the vessel into a *self-righteous* (or self-right), *self-justifying* container, it appears in the likeness of God, but the works that are brought forth are the works of satan. When people allow themselves to become distorted in their minds and cease to be honest and true to themselves, they live in hypocrisy. They then, and only then, become prepared and conformed vessels for the unrestricted use of the prince of this world (see Acts 5:1-5; Rom. 9:20-22):

> *And no marvel; for Satan himself is transformed into an angel of light. Therefore it is no great thing if his ministers also be transformed as the ministers of righteousness; whose end shall be according to their works* (2 Corinthians 11:14-15).

The Bible teaches that the desires of the flesh and (carnal) mind are the opposite of God's desires (see Eph. 2:3). For this reason, if people succumb to them, they become children of wrath. Jesus said, *"...That which is highly esteemed among **men** is abomination in the sight of God"* (Luke 16:15). The mind of the flesh, or carnal mind, is contrary to God, and therefore, is the enemy of God (see Rom. 8:6-7). As a result, God has cautioned His children to, *"Keep thy heart with all diligence; for out of it are the issues of life"* (Prov. 4:23).

Almost all sin is demon inspired and motivated, *but people can transgress of their own volition if they hold incorrect values in their hearts.* Eve was deceived by satan, but satan did not deceive Adam. Adam chose to disobey his Heavenly Father because he valued his wife's companionship and approval above God's (see 1 Tim. 2:14).

Satan became the god of this world when he overcame Adam through Eve. Adam had received dominion over all the earth (see Gen. 1:26-28; 2 Cor. 4:4). The Word of God states Jehovah made Moses a god to Pharaoh. Likewise, in the beginning Jehovah made Adam a god over all the world (see Exod. 7:1; John 10:34-35).

The devil coveted Adam's position of authority and went after it through Eve. Once she yielded to his lies, she was subject to him through sin. Then, because she was under his jurisdiction, when Adam yielded to her, he also came under satan's rule (see Rom. 6:16).

Satan used Eve to persuade Adam to submit to her and, thus, to himself, through her. In this way he was able to acquire the distinction of being the supreme ruler over God's creation (see Isa. 14:13-14).

When Adam sinned and brought all humanity under the dominion of satan, humanity became subject to satan and his demons through the Law of Dominion. When babies are born into this world, they become citizens of the world by birth. Because they are citizens, they are automatically under the jurisdiction of the one who rules the earth, *"the prince of the power of the air"* (Ps. 51:5; Eph. 2:2).

The Law of Sin

Paul said that he had a law in his members, warring against the law of his mind, bringing him *"into captivity to the law of sin"* that was in his members (see Rom. 7:23). The law of sin is one of the 12 Universal Laws of the Universe. It is partly defined in Romans 7:21: *"I find then a law, that when I would do good, evil is present with me."*

As children are born into this world, satan, through his demons, immediately begins an invasion process into each one's life. Although they are subjects of his empire at birth, they are not necessarily occupied by his troops. He must overthrow each one individually. He must deceive and conquer each child's free spirit and bring it under his control before he can take possession of the child's soul.

Satan accomplishes this conquest by hardening each child's heart, individually. As they mature and harden themselves against the adverse conditions and situations they encounter, trying to "make it through life," they fall into his snare (see Ps. 95:8-10; Dan. 5:20; Rom. 3:9-10).

Taking advantage of the reverse disposition of each child's flesh, satan works in and through it to bring each one into obedience (see James 1:14-15). First tempting, then deceiving, he provides apparent justification for each one to yield to sin. As adolescents are overcome by satan's deceptive tactics, they become hardened in their hearts to the mind of their spirits. Their flesh agrees with the devil, instead of agreeing with their conscience, because of the deceitful lust of their flesh (see 2 Cor. 11:3-4; Eph. 4:22). This natural tendency to agree with satan and sin is *the sin nature.*

Chapter 6

THE FORMATION OF THE SOUL

And the Lord God formed man of the dust of the ground, and breathed into his nostrils the breath of life; and man became a living soul (Genesis 2:7).

To understand the formation of the soul, we must examine the various components of which people are made. Medical science has discovered that an infant needs more than just the basic essentials of food, water, clothing, and shelter to grow up. Babies cannot achieve emotional maturity without someone administering proper emotional nourishment to them. If infants do not receive a certain amount of love and acceptance through someone holding and caring for them, their physical and mental well-being are adversely affected. To develop healthily, one must have both physical and spiritual nourishment.

From this simple observation, it is obvious that humans are more than just an earthly, physical creature. When people perceive themselves only as physical bodies, they omit the most important part of themselves—their spirits. Natural things, including the bodies of human beings, are temporary. Spiritual things are eternal (see Job 19:26).

Only spiritual things are everlasting. Even the earth, *"shall perish...and wax old as doth a garment...and shall be changed..."* (Heb. 1:10-12). People have a correct self-image only when they view themselves as eternal beings who will live either in Heaven or hell, forever:

And the Lord God formed man of the dust of the ground, and breathed into his nostrils the breath of life; and man became a living soul (Genesis 2:7).

The human spirit is eternal; the body is not. In the resurrection, people will receive an immortal house (body) to replace the temporal one, but even then it will be just a house. It will be a glorified, spiritual body, but a body, nonetheless (see 1 Cor. 15:44-50; 2 Cor. 5:1).

The Creator made the first Adam of dust. He then breathed a spirit into the body that He made and Adam *"became a living soul."* He was a soul, not just a body and not just a spirit, but a soul. Adam *"became"* a soul. He was the result of a body being made and a spirit being breathed (see Gen. 2:7).

Humanity is not just soil or dust. People *live in* an earthen house; they *have* a spirit and they *are* a soul. This is why the single word *"soul"* is equivalent to the whole person in many Scriptures (see Gen. 46:26; Exod. 1:5; Ezek. 18:20).

It is the merging of that which is earthly with that which is heavenly that creates the uniqueness of humanity. Much like an alloy consists of a composite of two dissimilar metals, humanity's soul is the consolidation of a heavenly spirit and an earthly body.

Hebrews 4:12 divides the body, soul, and spirit and in the process helps us understand their makeup. Although this verse does not mention the body or even the outer parts of the bones, it assumes their place in the soul's makeup. As the following illustration shows, the bones are symbolic of the body, the joints are symbolic of the soul, and the bone marrow represents the spirit.

For the word of God is quick, and powerful, and sharper than any two-edged sword, piercing even to the dividing asunder of soul and spirit, and of the joints and marrow, and is a discerner of the thoughts and intents of the heart (Hebrews 4:12).

THE BODY AND SPIRIT JOINED

FLESH   HEART

(BODY)
Soul & Spirit

(BONES)
Joints & Marrow

(DESIRES)
Thoughts & Intents

As seen in the chart above, the Scriptures compare one's soul to the joints of the bones. Without joints, the human body would be rigid. People's conscious thoughts, which make them flexible, are formed in their souls. Without thought, they would indeed be rigid, formal, legalistic, even robotic.

The Human soul, then, is the product of two different substances, one natural, one spiritual. All conscious thoughts are a product of these two. The *mind* of the spirit wars against the (subconscious) mind of the flesh, and the battle ground is the soul. The conscious mind, with its conscious thought, is an admixture of these two minds.

The *emotions* of the spirit, likewise, wrestle against their opponents— the emotions of the flesh—in the war-torn battleground of the soul. Decisions are made in the human soul (the conscious mind). Through conscious thought people decide which passions to allow to work in their members and which passions to deny.

For example, people are capable of allowing sensations of joy and feelings of happiness to proceed from their spirits into their conscious thoughts and be expressed through their souls (see Luke 10:21). On the other hand, if they so choose, they can express anger or even rejoice in iniquity, thereby taking pleasure in evil (see Rom. 1:32; 1 Cor. 13:6). Either way, the expression of their emotions is through their souls. The source of their feelings proceed either from their spirits or from their flesh and carnal minds.

The way one reacts to someone else's misfortune is another good example. People may experience sadness in their spirits because they love someone who is in pain, and they may express this with compassionate words and tears. On the negative side, if they harden their hearts and yield to the passions of their flesh and carnal minds, they may choose to inflict pain upon others. In extreme cases, they may even take pleasure in their sufferings (see Mark 1:41; Acts 7:54).

The Will

The soul has been incorrectly defined by many Christians as, *"the mind, the will, and the emotions."* The problem with this limited definition is that people have more than one will. The Bible even teaches that they have more than one mind. For instance, Paul said one could be spiritual-minded or carnal-minded. As we investigate the soul, we will discover that people have three minds, three wills, and at least two sets of emotions. In other words, the human spirit, soul, and body each have its own mind and will, and the spirit and body each have its own set of emotions.

In order to fully understand the human will, we must correctly divide the Word.[1] In variance to the doctrine that the soul consists of the mind, will, and emotions, Jesus said, *"...The spirit indeed is willing, but the flesh is weak"* (Matt. 26:41). For the spirit to be willing, it obviously has to have a will. But this is not the only will people have. John spoke of both the *"will of the flesh,"* and the *"will of man,"* yet he taught that people are not *"born again"* by either (see John 1:13).

Nevertheless, the fact that people's wills are directly involved in their salvation is confirmed by John's timeless invitation, *"...Whosoever will, let him take the water of life freely"* (Rev. 22:17). The will John was referring to in this verse is the will of the human spirit, which is the only acceptable will that humanity has. God looks on the heart and divides people's *conscious* wills from their *spirits'* wills (see 1 Sam. 16:7; Heb. 4:12). When people consciously yield to their spirits' hunger and thirst for righteousness and accept Christ's sacrificial offering on their behalf, they are born again. (Humanity's carnal mind is never willing to serve God; see Romans 8:7.)

Although the human spirit is quite willing to obey God, it is not in command—the soul is. The human soul is king, ruling people's lives, deciding their fates. *Every decision is finalized in the soul.* As a result, the soul determines whether people walk after the desires of their flesh and carnal mind (see Eph. 2:3) or after their spirits' will (see Heb. 4:12).

Paul said that God works, *"all things after the counsel of His own will"* (Eph. 1:11). God created the human spirit in His own likeness. When people listen to their spirits' counsel, they will usually make sound, reliable decisions. But when people refuse the counsel of their spirits and decide instead to fulfill the desires of their flesh and carnal minds, they will fall into sin.

Paul, speaking from the viewpoint of a carnal man under the Law, said that although he desired to do good, he found himself being drawn into sin against his will. He said the lust of his flesh prevailed over the will of his spirit. When he was under the Law, he was weak and unable to perform the intent (will) of his spirit. His spirit nudged him with the desire to do right, but the deceitful lusts that proceeded from his carnal mind overpowered him and brought him into sin (see Rom. 7:1,7-9,9-25).

At the risk of being redundant, let me repeat: The expression of the soul's will is invariably in the form of a decision. Whenever people are tempted, their actions or reactions, whether in word or deed, are determined by the conscious decisions their souls make. Their decisions are always the result of their spirits' counsel *or* the results of their flesh and carnal minds' lustful desires. God's Spirit works in conjunction with their spirits, influencing them to make good and righteous decisions (see Rom. 1:9). On the other hand, satan influences people through the desires of their flesh and carnal minds, prompting them to please their flesh (see Eph. 2:2-3). Either way, the selections they make may be called their *self-will.*

People are responsible for the choices they make. God holds them accountable because they can, consciously, through their thoughts, choose between their spirits' will and their carnal desires (see Isa. 1:19-20; Rev. 22:17). Paul explained further in Romans 8:13 that if people choose to live after the lust of their flesh and carnal minds, they will die. To avoid this, people should view themselves as eternal people living temporarily in an earthen house. By allowing the minds of their spirits to stay focused on spiritual things, they will live. Furthermore, they will not fulfill the lust of their flesh (see Gal. 5:16).

The Formation of the Soul

The development of Adam's soul occurred as he became aware of his surroundings and began exercising his senses to discern (know) good and evil (see Heb. 5:14). Through his experiences he developed various attitudes, opinions, habits, and conditioned responses. He received all the intellectual and emotional awareness and training that make up a personality, or soul, through his experiences.

There are several factors that work to condition and shape the soul. These things mold people's personalities into very diverse, yet predictable patterns. All the elements that influence the development of the soul were evident in the Garden of Eden.

First, *Environment* has a direct influence upon people's development. If there had not been a tree of knowledge of good and evil in the garden, Eve would not have been tempted by its fruit (see Gen. 2:9).

Second, *Relationships* greatly contribute to the forming of people's personalities. Family role models, personal training, and even inherited traits such as beauty and intelligence all contribute to the soul's development. If Adam had been alone, his inherent desire to please God would have been sufficient to prevent him from sinning. He was not deceived. His natural desire to please was directed toward Eve, and in pleasing her, he failed to please God (see 1 Cor. 7:32-33; Gal. 1:10).

Adam's incorrect attitude toward his wife contributed directly to his error in judgment, which led to his disobedience. Adam was influenced through his relationship with Eve because his values were wrong. Because of this, his companion played a major role in his downfall (see 1 Cor. 7:29,32-34, 15:33).

Third, if *satan* had not *tempted* Adam's wife to sin, Adam would not have been influenced by her example of wrongdoing (see 2 Cor. 11:3). Likewise, if satan did not tempt Adam's descendants, they would not be as prone to sin either.

Fourth, if *God* had not withdrawn *the consciousness of His presence* during the time of Adam's temptation, satan's lie would have been instantly contradicted by the Spirit of Truth. God's intervention would have prevented the whole chain of events that led to Adam's downfall (see Gen. 3:8, 6:3; 1 John 3:9). The consciousness of God's presence, through spiritual experiences, church attendance, or simply the godly (or ungodly) example of people's parents or grandparents is very influential in forming children's personalities.

Fifth, Adam's *own decision* to sin when he yielded to the temptation to harken (submit) to his wife was also a contributing factor in his trespass (see 2 Tim. 4:10). Likewise, people's decisions ultimately determine the final form of their character and personality.

Although we have only examined the evolution of the sinful disposition of people, these same five things also control the development of the virtuous side of people's personalities. The factors are the same, whether the situations and circumstances people are fashioned by bring forth righteousness or iniquity in their lives.

These five fundamental factors—environment, relationships, satan's temptations, God's intervention (through conviction, training, example, or inheritance; see 2 Timothy 1:5), and one's own decisions—mold the lives and shape the souls of all people as they move from adolescence to maturity. Their personalities are formed as they react to these five influences in their own strengths and weaknesses.

As children develop, their gender, physical size and strength, intelligence, and personality (stubborn or submissive nature) all help sway their decisions one way or the other. These things are very influential in forming their decisions and reactions to the countless circumstances and relationships in which they find themselves.

Role Models

Role models play a very important part in the development of children's souls. Toddlers' hearts are easily molded by the examples of others. Although words play an important part in their growth, children's abilities to observe and learn from the activities of others influence them to a far greater degree than the words they hear. Children do as they see people do, not as people say.

Children's first *"god"* is their parents. In truth, infants are created by their parents—in them infants lived before conception and birth, and by them infants live after birth (see Heb. 7:9-10; Acts 17:28). Children's parents exercise supreme control over their lives for the first few years. If their parents care for them, feed them, clothe and shelter them, they live. If they deny them the basic essentials of life, whether physical or emotional, they perish.

When parents say or do something to small children, the little ones believe that whatever the adults say or do is right. Their spirits, which are created in the likeness of God, know instinctively that God cannot lie (see Rom. 2:14-15). When children are small, their parents are *"god"* to them; therefore, they accept whatever they say or do as truth.

For example, when parents give a 2-year-old daughter a gift at Christmas and tell her Santa Claus brought it, she does not question the validity of the statement. Likewise, if a father tells a small son that a bogeyman is in the dark, because he is believed, the little boy's heart is opened to a spirit of fear.

As the girl grows older and her mind matures, she learns there is no Santa Claus, and there is seldom any real harm as a result. The spirit of fear, however, does not leave the boy just because he learns bogeymen do not exist. This spirit has to be overcome and expelled in one way or another for the child to have peace and be without undue fear of darkness.

Children have no way of knowing right from wrong or good from evil when they are very young (see Isa. 7:16; Heb. 5:14). As their souls are formed, incorrect images, examples, and words received in early years often allow satan into their flesh to distort the formation of their character.

For example, if a young boy is rejected by his parents, he receives an indelible message recorded in his heart that he is a reject. His innocent spirit does not know to resist the erroneous message given to him by his parent's words and deeds. Whenever he is rejected, a spirit of rejection takes advantage of the situation and enters him. As he matures he has both the erroneous message and the unclean spirit to contend with. As he grows older, some of the faulty images, untrue statements, and wrong examples are corrected as he struggles to stay upright in his spirit. Some are not. Those that have taken root and are not uprooted will one day bring forth bitter fruit in his life (see Heb. 12:15).

Endnote

1. Ira L. Milligan, *Rightly Dividing the Word* (Tioga, LA: Servant Ministries, Inc., 2000), 83-87.

Chapter 7

THE MIND'S SPIRIT VERSUS THE SPIRIT'S MIND

The eight basic desires of the flesh and carnal mind constantly oppose and contradict the will and intent of the spirit. *The spirit of the carnal mind is diametrically opposed to the mind of the spirit (conscience)* (see Rom. 2:15, 7:25, 8:5-7; Eph. 4:23). To exercise dominion over sin, people must lay the axe of God's Word to the roots of the tree of sin. They must take their own thoughts, words, and deeds captive (see Matt. 12:37; Rom. 6:14, 8:13; 2 Cor. 10:5):

> *And now also the axe is laid unto the root of the trees: every tree therefore which bringeth not forth good fruit is hewn down, and cast into the fire* (Luke 3:9).

The roots of the tree of sin are **attitudes**. An attitude is the *significance* or *value* people place on something. Attitudes are the basis for the opinions people form and, therefore, the basis for the many decisions that they must make in life. It is easy to see that people's opinions govern many facets of their lives.

The branches of the tree of sin are people's motives. The fruits (sins) of the tree are the deeds they perform as they try to satisfy the desires of their flesh and carnal minds (see Rom. 7:5). Jesus said: *"Either make the tree good, and his fruit good; or else make the tree corrupt, and his fruit corrupt..."* (Matt. 12:33).

As people reevaluate their lives in agreement with God's Word and *change their attitudes,* they change their thoughts (and their words). Then, because their thoughts are oriented toward things above, their actions and deeds are changed from sinful responses to righteous ones (see Rom. 6:16-19; Col. 3:2-4).

People cannot obey James 4:7 (resist the devil) consistently, until they are willing to deal properly with the root attitudes of their hearts. They must recondition their worldly thinking to conform to God's Word before they can walk in righteousness (see Prov. 16:3; Isa. 55:7-9). John warned the young people of his day about maintaining a right attitude toward the world:

> *Love not the world, neither the things that are in the world. If any man love the world, the love of the Father is not in him. For all that is in the world, the lust of the flesh, and the lust of the eyes, and the pride of life, is not of the Father, but is of the world* (1 John 2:15-16).

As usual, Jesus' words were even more direct: *"...That which is highly esteemed among men is abomination in the sight of God"* (Luke 16:15). Paul also admonished his followers to develop correct values. He exhorted them to set their affections on things above, not on things on this earth. Before people can do this, they must first adopt the attitude that only eternal things are precious. As long as people cherish temporary gain or pleasure, they will be drawn toward it (see Phil. 3:7-8). Jesus said that people's hearts would be wherever their treasure is (see Matt. 6:21).[1] People's hearts are fixed upon and drawn toward whatever they esteem as precious.

If people's attitudes are wrong, they will resist the minds of their own spirits. Hardening their hearts toward their consciences, they will carry out their lustful desires instead of their spiritual, or righteous, preferences (see Rom. 7:18-19; Heb. 3:8-10). For instance, Eve did not sin until she was deceived. Adam did not sin until convinced to do so by Eve. His attitude toward her, in relation to his attitude toward God, was wrong. As a result, he *"harkened"* to his wife (see Gen. 3:17). He valued her companionship and counsel more than God's. Satan did not deceive Adam—his incorrect attitude caused him to choose wrong and sin:

> *Every way of a man is right in his own eyes...But there is a way that seemeth right unto a man, but the end thereof are the ways of death* (Proverbs 21:2, 16:25).

The Spirit of Truth

To aid His children in this inner warfare, God has given them His Spirit. The spirit of error is directly contradicted by the Spirit of Truth, which God has given to those who obey Him (see Acts 5:32):

> *And when* [the Spirit of Truth] *is come, He will reprove the world of sin, and of righteousness, and of judgment* (John 16:8).

Proper convictions come when the *Spirit of Truth* (as opposed to the evil *prince of this world*) gives people revelation knowledge through the Word. God's Word is truth. *Proper convictions consist of true knowledge of good and evil, with the correct attitude (judgment) toward each.* Truth is the knowledge of sin (evil), of righteousness (good), and judgment (attitude), in proper balance (see Rom. 16:19-20; Phil. 1:9-10).

Because renewal of the mind is a work of the Holy Spirit, renewal brings conviction of sin, righteousness, and judgment. Sin is doing wrong, righteousness is doing that which is right, and judgment is the proper attitude toward right and wrong (see 1 John 2:15, 3:7,10).

Renewal of the mind causes people to abhor sin and love righteousness. Also, renewal of the mind gives them the proper attitude toward themselves, their relationships with other people, and their material possessions (see Matt. 23:23; John 16:8-11; Rev. 12:10-11).

Convictions are the walls of defense people's spirits erect against the spirit of this world! Faith overcomes the world. Conviction is the essence of faith (see 1 John 5:4; Heb. 11:1). Jesus said:

> *I can of Mine own self do nothing: as I hear, I judge: and My judgment is just; because I seek not Mine own will, but the will of the Father which hath sent Me* (John 5:30).

As this Scripture shows, correct attitude (judgment) toward good and evil comes from *"hearing"* God's Word. The Word of God is truth (proper knowledge and attitude), and the truth makes people free (see John 8:31-32).

Jesus' words reveal that wrong judgments proceed from wrong desires. Peter opposed Jesus when he heard Him teach what he thought was false doctrine. When Peter rejected the idea that Jesus was going to be crucified, Jesus rebuked him. He said that Peter's error, and his consequential rebuke, came from savoring the things of the world:

> *But He* [Jesus] *turned, and said unto Peter, Get thee behind Me, Satan: thou art an offense unto Me: for thou savourest not the things that be of God, but those that be of men* (Matthew 16:23).

Peter's attitude was wrong. God desires and requires truth in the inner person, in the soul:

> *Behold, Thou desirest truth in the inward parts: and in the hidden part Thou shalt make me to know wisdom* (Psalm 51:6).

As we explore each of the eight categories of sin, we will look in detail at each desire, or lust, and its motivating attitude (root). An understanding of wrong attitudes is essential for mastering the scorpion within humanity.

Endnote

1.   For more on this, see the Law of Worship, in the endnotes of Chapter 3 (pages 32-33).

Chapter 8

RATTLESNAKE RODEO

In time past ye walked according to the course of this world, according to the prince of the power of the air, the spirit that now worketh in the children of disobedience: Among whom also we all had our conversation in times past in the lusts of our flesh, fulfilling the desires of the flesh and of the mind; and were by nature the children of wrath, even as others (Ephesians 2:2-3).

Satan, as the prince of the power of the air, commands four levels of demon forces. These demons are sent forth into the earth to invade, conquer, and occupy all humanity. The four ranks of demons are listed in Ephesians 1:20-21:

Christ [is]...Far above all principality, and power, and might, and dominion, and every name that is named... (Ephesians 1:20-21).

1. Principality (rule, chief in time, place, rank, or order)

2. Power (authority)

3. Might (miracle power)

4. Dominion (mastery)

Humanity's primary warfare is against the first two—*principalities*, the rulers of darkness, and *powers*, the demons that gain authority to perform mischief (see Ps. 94:20; Eph. 6:12; Col. 2:13-15).

Principalities (Rulers)

A principality is a demon spirit that influences people's minds with incorrect, worldly ideas and attitudes. By displacing and replacing the righteous counsel of people's spirits, this demon supplies seemingly good and logical reasons for why he is right and their consciences are wrong (see Gen. 3:4-5). His purpose is to persuade people to yield to the power (authority) that works with him, the demon who begins the actual work of sin in people's members.

A principality rules the spirits under him (including the spirits of humans, when captured by him). He rules people's spirits primarily through deception and falsehood (see Prov. 25:28; 2 Cor. 11:3-4; 2 Tim. 2:26).

There are eight principalities. Each principality persuades people to believe and agree with him either through reasoning, imagination, emotion, or memory. There are two principalities who use reasoning, two who stimulate the imagination, two who arouse (or suppress) the emotions, and two who prod the memory, activating conditioned responses in the process. One pair works primarily through the spirit, one pair through the passions of the flesh, one pair through the carnal mind, and one pair through the soul. (We will discuss this in greater detail as we progress.)

People's consciences instinctively challenge a principality's deceitful persuasion, but once people are convinced and agree with him, the resistance ceases. Although people's spirits naturally reject this demon, their carnal minds are predisposed to agree with him (see Rom. 8:7; Gal. 5:17). Paul was admonishing Christians to combat principalities in Ephesians 4:23, *"And be renewed in the spirit of your mind."*

Powers (Authorities)

A power demon exercises authority over people who are under a principality's evil influence. This spirit works primarily through compulsive or impulsive desires. By using these obsessions he can bring about unreasonable, illogical, selfish behavior within his victims (see James 3:15-16). The *imagination* is greatly used by this evil spirit.

Mights (Miracle Powers)

The might (Greek: *dunamis*)[1] of the spirit world can then be seen in the third step of this relentless process of demonic invasion. The miracle power, or *might*, of satan's forces compels people into sin. No longer capable of resisting within their own will, they are drawn into sin through the passions (*emotions*) and lusts working in their members (see Rom. 7:23).

Once people have yielded their members to iniquity, they are bound by the cords of their sin: *"His own iniquities shall take the wicked himself, and he shall be holden with the cords of his sins"* (Prov. 5:22). Through the addictive power of passion, the Law of Dominion becomes a nightmarish reality in the lives of this spirit's victims:

> *Know ye not, that to whom ye yield yourselves servants to obey,*
> *his servants ye are to whom ye obey; whether of sin unto death,*
> *or of obedience unto righteousness?* (Romans 6:16)

Dominions (Masteries)

Finally, people are brought into the fullness of iniquity in each separate area of their personalities by a dominion spirit. This foul spirit's goal is to gain total control over each person's life. When people yield their members to this evil spirit, their souls are taken captive. This demon exercises mastery over their thoughts to completely control their lives in each sin category, respectively (see 2 Tim. 2:25-26).

A dominion is a spirit that produces a certain manner of thinking, or *"manner of spirit,"* in the conscious mind. These thought patterns condition people to react to certain circumstances in specific ways. This conditioning (training) brings forth predictable, habitual behavior, or *conditioned responses,* under given conditions or stimuli. The *memory,* both conscious and subconscious, is primarily used by this demon (see Luke 9:54-55).

Each of the eight spirits of dominion work to open people's hearts and condition their minds to believe and receive the next principality. Each dominion spirit that obtains mastery over people's minds generates certain thoughts and sensations that make them susceptible to the next principality. This succession of demonic invaders enables the forces of satan to intrude deeper and deeper into each victim's life (see 2 Tim. 3:13).

Every Name Under Heaven

In identifying the four ranks of demon forces, Paul concluded the list with, *"...and every name that is named"* (Eph. 1:21).

Demons are named two ways. One method of identifying them is by their character, such as evil or wicked. There are five names given in the scriptures that are common to all demons. These are: *evil, wicked, seducing, unclean,* and *foul* (see Matt. 12:45; Acts 19:13; 1 Tim. 4:1).

For example, Jesus called a demon that He cast out of a deaf boy by several different names. In Luke, He called the demon an *unclean* spirit (see Luke 9:42). Mark recalled that He also called the same spirit a *dumb* spirit, a *foul* spirit, and a *dumb and deaf* spirit (see Mark 9:17,25).

A second way of naming demons is by what they do. In the same manner that we call a man who works with building materials (lumber, saws, hammer, and nails) a carpenter, a demon who works hatred in the hearts of its victims is called a spirit of hate. Likewise, a demon who causes people to grieve is known as a spirit of grief.

There may be several different names for each unclean spirit. For example, one can also identify a spirit of grief by its biblical name, *"the spirit of heaviness,"* or by some of the emotions that it stimulates in its victims—mourning, sadness, depression, etc. (see Isa. 61:3).

Besides the obvious feelings the different names already listed suggest, a spirit of grief may also manifest himself in people by making them weep or feel lonesome. Feelings of dismay and discouragement, along with sensations of hopelessness and despair, are also common ways this spirit expresses himself. Feelings and thoughts of self-pity are usually very familiar to people who have a spirit of grief.

Depending upon the area of the flesh that he has invaded and occupied, any given spirit will manifest himself in different ways through different people. For example, a spirit of anger may exhibit himself through one personality type by violent acts, slamming doors, throwing objects, or even striking people. Also, abusive words and cursing are common expressions of a demon of anger. Yet, in another personality type this same spirit may cause his victim to sulk and refuse to speak to someone for several days or even years (see 1 Sam. 20:30-31,34).

An unclean spirit will reveal himself in a specific way through one person; but if he is cast out and invades another, he may reveal himself in a totally different way. Jesus said that when an unclean spirit is cast out of a person he seeks another individual to live in if he cannot reenter the person from whom he was expelled (see Luke 11:24-26). When he finds a new victim, he must create a way to manifest himself through that person. His specific work and his new name—but not his nature—will depend upon the area of the poor victim's personality that he manages to invade. (His nature never changes.)

A good example of a spirit with many different names is the spirit of anxiety. The same spirit that makes one person afraid of the dark (achluophobia) will make another fear drowning (hydrophobia), or will cause another to shudder at the thought of being locked in a small place (claustrophobia). The same spirit works through the carnal mind and generates different responses in different people; therefore, he is known by many different names.

In the same manner, a spirit of whoredoms will manifest himself through the specific personality of the one he has invaded (see Hos. 5:4). In one person he may produce the evil fruit of homosexuality, but in another, adultery (see Matt. 7:18-20).

Demons sow their seed in people, and the harvest that is reaped is sin (see Matt. 13:24-25,39; Luke 3:7-9). Jesus said His followers would know false prophets by their fruits. Likewise, the spirits who dwell in them are known by their fruits. Demons are deceitful. As a result, people must learn to properly identify them by their fruits (works) and not just by the feelings or thoughts they cause people to have (see Matt. 7:15-17; 1 John 3:8).

Rage, hate, anger, and disgust all feel very much alike; yet, all these feelings are produced through the emotions by several different spirits at different times. In contrast to this, a person who kills another human being may feel rage, anger, lust, or greed, or he may be deliberate and unemotional. Yet, the spirit compelling him to murder is usually the same as in all other murderers—hatred (see Gen. 4:5-8; 2 Sam. 3:27, 11:14-17; Acts 7:54-59; 1 John 3:15).

In summary, it is important to note that all demons, whether heaviness, anxiety, whoredoms, hate, or any other unclean spirit, work in different ways through different people. They manifest themselves to and through people by different obsessions and sensations using a wide variety of names.

It is this diversity of names and manifestations (feelings and works) that has led to so much confusion in the area of deliverance in the past. There has been much *fruit picking*, with the disappointing results of a later crop of evil fruits when the next *season* came around. To stop this ongoing process, the axe must be laid to the root of the problem, not the fruit. *If the axe is laid to the root, the tree of sin will die, and the fruit will not reappear.*

This is not to imply that it is not important to know the area of the personality over which an evil spirit has obtained victory. It is this knowledge that enables people to liberate themselves and to defend themselves against a spirit's return.

Without a correct understanding of wrong attitudes and actions, people are unable to repent properly. People yield themselves to the subterfuge of their enemy through ignorance of his devices (see 2 Cor. 2:11). It is also ignorance that makes them subject to the return of his invading forces. The truth (knowledge) alone gives freedom. By amending incorrect actions and improper patterns of thought, people can free themselves from satan and escape the corruption that is in the world through lust (see Isa. 55:7; John 8:32; Acts 2:40).

There are eight categories of sin. There are four demons in each sin category. These 32 demons are properly identified by their works. If people know their works, and how they work, then they can wage effective spiritual warfare. Satan, the spirit of this world, uses these 32 demons to supplant, or displace, the human spirit. His goal is to bring people's thoughts and, therefore, their words and actions, under total demonic control (see Acts 5:3).

As we have previously discussed, people's thoughts are formulated in their souls, but generated by their bodies or spirits. When people's thoughts are initiated by their spirits, they are spiritual minded. If their thoughts are initiated by the passions of the flesh and the ambitions of the subconscious, carnal mind, they are carnal minded. *When people are deceived by demons through their sin nature and are carnal minded, they are subject to satan's invasion, manipulation, and control* (see Rom. 8:5-7).

The Wheel of Nature

The Bible refers to this process of demonic invasion as *"the cycle* [or wheel] *of man's nature"*:

> *And the tongue is a fire. The tongue is a world of wickedness set among our members, contaminating and depraving the whole body and setting on fire **the wheel of** birth—the cycle of man's **nature**—being itself ignited by hell...* (James 3:6 AMP).

James revealed that satan uses the process of iniquity to give the *Wheel of Nature* its rotational force (*see the illustration on the following page*). We will discuss the Wheel of Nature in greater detail later, building each segment one at a time. Students will see the importance of understanding this wheel as they learn to identify and disarm the enemy of the soul.

People disarm principalities and powers by annulling satan's covenant of sin. When people are in covenant agreement with demons, they are subject to them. *Once they repent, confess their sins, and renounce satan's lies, he is disarmed* (see Prov. 28:13; 2 Cor. 4:2). Then demons lose their power and are subject to people through their covenant with God (see Gen. 22:17; Exod. 23:22,27; Luke 10:19).

Endnote

1.   All references to Greek word definitions are from *Strong's Exhaustive Concordance,* Thomas Nelson Publishers, 1990.

The Wheel of Nature

Chapter 9

SPIRIT, SOUL, AND BODY

M oses, Paul, John, and the unknown writer of Hebrews all refer to the three parts of man (see Gen. 2:7; Heb. 4:12; 3 John 2). Paul said, *"...I pray God your whole spirit and soul and body be preserved blameless at the coming of our Lord Jesus Christ"* (1 Thess. 5:23). We will now examine the human spirit, soul, and body and how they function in relation to demons.

> *Wherein in time past ye walked according to the course of this world, according to the prince of the power of the air, the spirit that now worketh in the children of disobedience. Among whom also we all had our conversation in times past in the lusts of our flesh, fulfilling the desires of the flesh and of the mind; and were by nature the children of wrath, even as others* (Ephesians 2:2-3).

Flesh's Desire

The primary expression of the desires of the flesh can be simply stated in one word—*passion*. The passions of human flesh motivate people to possess the things of this world. They use their five senses to obtain intimate knowledge of all they find pleasurable.

The things they lust for may be tangible or intangible, animate or inanimate. For example, some people may desire their neighbors' land, house, car, boat, or wealth, while others may covet their neighbors' spouse. Human passions draw many to such things as sensuous music, dancing, and drinking alcohol or even vile, perverted sex acts and pornography. Enjoyable fragrances, which are pleasant to the sense of smell, through conditioned responses, also have the power to excite evil imaginations and passions in men.

People's natural passions, properly controlled and fulfilled, are harmless, innocent, and pure (see Tit. 1:15). On the other hand, unbridled passions cause people to become immoral, thieves, con artists, or even such things as cruel rapists and murderers. Human passions inflamed by demons are often so strong that people are driven to satisfy their evil lusts even at the expense of their own families or friends.

Mind's Desire

Just as the flesh's desires can be briefly stated in the word *passion*, the desires of the body's carnal mind can also be summed up in one word—*power*. People attempt to satisfy their lust for power in many different ways. For example, some strive to obtain power through prestigious positions while others struggle for power by trying to develop a special reputation among their peers (see Gen. 10:9-10).

Worldly knowledge is frequently used as a source of power. Knowing more than the neighbors often enables people to obtain promotions and positions above them or to earn special favors. Knowledge may also enable people to earn more money, another common source of power (see Eccl. 10:19).

Paul's familiar statement, *"The love of money is the root of all evil"* (which we will discuss later) shows that the desire for worldly knowledge and the ability to become wealthy through knowledge have many hidden snares (see 1 Tim. 6:7-10).

The carnal lust for power and control was in the early church just as it is today. The apostle John wrote of one man who desired to have pre-eminence among his peers. This man even threw those who dared to disagree with him out of the church (see 3 John 9-10). We have already seen how this desire for power led to satan's downfall (see Isa. 14:12-15). Beware of him, because he uses the same, subtle snare on men that he fell for in the beginning. He coveted the authority and power that God gave Adam. He worked through Eve because she was gullible and totally unprepared for his deceitful attack. He is still deceiving many unsuspecting victims the same way today.

In direct opposition to this carnal lust, Jesus *"made himself of no reputation"* (Phil. 2:7). He resisted all natural and spiritual ambition and subdued the desires of His carnal mind, placing them under the will of His Father (see John 6:15):

> *For to be carnally minded is death…Because the carnal mind is enmity against God: for it is not subject to the law of God, neither indeed can be* (Romans 8:6-7).

The carnal mind is a subconscious mind. It is God's hidden enemy. The conscious mind of man is not the enemy of God. The conscious mind is the mind of the soul. When it is in harmony with the spirit, it is used to pray, praise, witness, and do many other activities which are subject to God's Law. It is the subconscious, carnal mind that is antagonistic toward God. It will not *and cannot* obey His Law (see Rom. 8:7).

Spirit's Intent (Will)

As we have already discussed, *the human acceptable will is in the spirit* (see Matt. 26:41; Mark 14:38; Rom. 1:9, 7:16-20). Jesus said that the human spirit is ready and willing to please and serve God. The human spirit also desires to please and serve other people (within the bounds of conscience).

69

Hebrews 4:12 uses the word *intent* in place of the word *will* when referring to the human spirit. Although the spirit's intentions may be right and good and even perfectly clear, without God's help, people are incapable of performing their spirits' will because of the weakness of their flesh and the hardness of their hearts (see Matt. 26:41; John 1:13; 1 Pet. 4:3; 2 Pet. 1:21; Rev. 22:17).

God works, *"all things after the counsel of His own will"* (Eph. 1:11). What He intends to do is what He does (see Isa. 46:10). His soul, being free from the negative influence of a carnal body, consistently plans and executes the will (intent) of His Spirit (see Matt. 12:18).

Likewise, Jesus never allowed His flesh to dominate His soul. All the works that He did were according to the counsel of His own Spirit, which is the Spirit of God (see John 14:10, 20:28; 2 Cor. 5:19; 1 Tim. 3:16). In His soul He always chose to accomplish the intent of His Spirit. He did not allow the desires of His flesh and carnal mind to determine His words or deeds (see Matt. 26:38-39; Luke 4:1-13; Phil. 2:3-8; Heb. 4:15).

Christians should follow His example. People's spirits counsel them in accordance with their inherent character, or nature, which is the same as God's nature. Every soul is responsible to listen to and act in agreement with the counsel of its own conscience. God made people's spirits in His own likeness, and because they are a true representation of His will, He requires people to obey their spirits (see Acts 24:16; James 4:17).

When the human spirit is free from deception and the defilement of the consciousness of sin (guilt), people normally will not sin (see Heb. 9:14). The human conscience is enough to keep people from sinning if their attitudes are right (see Gen. 3:2-3).

The counsel of the human conscience (the mind of the human spirit) is like a compass in the hands of a wise woodsman. It gives clear, consistent directions directing people toward what is good and away from things that are wrong. When followed, these directions lead people to obey the Universal Law of Love, otherwise known as the Universal Law of Righteousness (see Rom. 2:14-15, 13:9-10; Gal. 5:14).

The Law of Sin—"*When I would do good, evil is present with me*" (Rom. 7:21)—is counteracted by the Law of Love—*When I would do evil, good is present with me*—which is the conviction of the conscience. This Law is recorded in every person's heart from birth by the nature of the spirit (see Matt. 18:3-4; Rom. 2:14-15).

This is the reason people can choose or reject salvation. When they hear the Gospel, they can decide to believe, or they can choose unbelief. If they believe, they are made free from the Law of Sin and Death. By submitting themselves to God's authority and rule, they become free. Jesus was not deceived. He never once submitted Himself to sin. He totally defeated satan and the flesh; as a result, He is completely free. *Through the Law of Dominion, when people submit themselves to Christ's Lordship, they are made free because their Master is free* (see John 8:34-36; Rom. 8:2).

Of course, people are also free to decide not to believe. Faith is the result of a decision. If people exercise faith it is because they *elected* to hear their consciences and believe. To decide not to hear is unbelief. The fact that people can choose or refuse to hear makes them accountable. This is also the reason Jesus rebuked people for their unbelief (see Matt. 8:26, 14:31, 16:8, 17:17). People usually think of the conscience only in the negative sense of correcting them when they have done wrong. The conscience also has a positive function. It convicts people concerning truth and righteousness. Therefore, faith is also by the conscience (see Heb. 11:1; 1 Pet. 3:21).

Paul said that his conscience bore witness to the truthfulness and righteousness of his conduct (see Rom. 9:1). People's consciences either convict them of wrongdoing or lead them into righteousness by faith. When people's consciences confirm them in righteousness, they have confidence toward God (see 1 John 3:21).

The conscience is a counselor, not a dictator, so it cannot keep people from sinning. The human spirit warns people when they are being tempted and accuses them after they have sinned. Because people's perception of a warning is different from an accusation (a warning is not accompanied with strong feelings of condemnation), the spirit's warning sometimes goes unheeded. After people sin, however, when their spirits accuse and reprove them of wrongdoing, it is both felt and heard (see 1 Sam. 24:4-5; 2 Sam. 24:10).

The difference in the way the spirit advises and warns people and the way it accuses them after they have sinned is the reason people sometimes sin before they realize they were being warned. But people's spirits begin cautioning them against evil when they first start thinking about doing wrong.

The human spirit is the *counselor* before people sin and the *judge* after they sin. People's spirits cannot condemn them while they are just being tempted (temptation is not a sin). Their spirits must wait until they are in the actual process of sinning or even after the deed has been performed before they can convict them. Then the spirits' *"I told you so"* judgment is offensive to people. Because of people's pride and passion, they often harden their hearts against their spirits' conviction (see John 8:7-9; 1 Cor. 11:31-32).

The flesh and carnal mind are influenced by, *"the counsel of the ungodly"* (Ps. 1:1). Satan pressures people with logical reasoning, vivid images, passionate feelings, and sweet (or even bitter) memories to entice them into sin (see John 13:2). The soft, intuitive feelings and sensations of the human spirit must be enlightened and confirmed by the Word of God (or the Spirit of Truth) to overcome the flesh's powerful thoughts and feelings. The expressions which proceed from carnal lusts must be overcome by the Word and Spirit of Truth (see Luke 4:2-14; John 6:63).

When people are mature, the confirming voice of the Spirit of Truth is necessary before they can consistently overcome their carnal nature (see Gen. 6:3). *The Holy Spirit speaks before people sin, convicting them of wrong judgments.* Through the Spirit of Truth, people know the truth, but not just the truth concerning sin—they also know the truth concerning righteousness. In this way, God provides the *"how to"* that people cannot find when they are under the dominion of the Law of Sin (see John 16:8-13; Rom.

7:18,23). When people become sensitive and responsive to the influence of God's Spirit, He provides the truth necessary to overcome the wrong persuasions of the deceiver (see John 8:31-32).

The Soul's Thought

As we previously discussed, our soul is the product of joining our body with our spirit. Our soul incorporates impressions from our flesh, carnal mind, and spirit to form our conscious thoughts. Then we express them with words and actions.

All decisions are made in the soul. By taking the information received through the five senses of the body and the images and feelings received from the carnal mind, people form their conscious thoughts and words in their souls. They also incorporate the intuitive knowledge of the spirit (expressed to the soul through images, sensations, and feelings) into their decision-making process.

Attitudes, which are best defined as people's *values*, are also a product of the soul. The soul's values form the basis for the opinions people hold and the decisions they make.

People's actions and reactions result from the decisions the soul makes (or in the case of conditional responses, decisions that were previously made). It is through the soul that the body is consciously controlled. All willful activity is a direct expression of the soul. Solomon said, *"Keep thy heart with all diligence; for out of it are the issues of life"* (Prov. 4:23).

The human heart consists of the spirit and soul together (see Heb. 4:12). It is in the heart that people struggle with balancing the lust for passion and power with the righteous intents of their spirits. The principal instrument for achieving this is intuitive reasoning and imagination.

The soul is a part of the heart and can yield to the desires of the flesh or the will of the spirit. As a result, in the Bible the heart is called both good and evil. The heart is sometimes spoken of in the Scriptures as being deceitful, wicked, blind, hard, and evil (see Jer. 17:9; Eph. 4:18; Heb. 3:10-15).

The human spirit is also a part of the heart. As a result, when appropriate, the Scriptures speak of the heart as being pure, honest, and good (see Matt. 5:8; Luke 8:15). The determining factor as to whether the heart is considered evil or good is whether people are carnally or spiritually minded.

Satan's Intent

Satan's expressed desire is to elevate himself and be like God (see Isa. 14:12-14). To accomplish his purpose, he must have a body. Because he does not have one of his own, he endeavors to use people's bodies. To accomplish his ambition, he must obtain authority (dominion or mastery) over God's creation, bringing people into service and obedience to him in thought, word, and deed (see Ps. 94:20; Rom. 6:16).

Satan's Tactic

Satan's tactic is to subdue each human's spirit, replacing its counsel with his own. By working through the spirit of the carnal mind (see Eph. 4:23), he uses such things as *intuitive* reasoning along with vain imaginations and strong passions and feelings to tempt and motivate people to sin. He persuades them through their conscious minds, justifying them in disobeying God's Law by using logical reasoning (with lies). His objective is to confuse, deceive, and blind them. His goal is to achieve his evil ambition at their expense (see Prov. 16:2; 2 Cor. 4:4; James 1:14-15).

Satan's Purpose

Jesus said satan was a *thief* and that his purpose was to *steal, kill,* and *destroy* God's works (see John 10:10). This is also revealed in satan's four primary natures.

The Four Natures of Satan

Tempter

The *first* designated nature of the *thief* is that he is a *tempter.* Working through people's senses and using people's own passions, he discreetly stimulates their feelings and tempts them with imaginations of sinful pleasures. His goal is to entice them to yield to sin so that he can obtain authority to spoil their goods (see 1 Thess. 3:5; James 1:14; 1 John 2:16).

Deceiver

The *second* nature of satan is to *deceive.* Through deceptive reasoning, lies, and self-justification, the thief labors to *steal* the use of people's bodies. By suppressing the human spirit, he tries to use people's flesh and minds to please himself at their expense (see 2 Cor. 10:5; Rev. 12:9).

Accuser

The *third* nature of satan is to *accuse.* By accusing people before God, *through the brethren,* the murdering thief strives to take their lives, both natural and spiritual. Through his deception, he tries to get people to accuse one another, trying to *kill* them with their own words! *"For by thy words thou shalt be justified, and by thy words thou shalt be condemned"* (Matt. 12:37). Using self-justification, scorn, and envy, the *"accuser of the brethren"* makes people think they are right in criticizing others. He kills them with their own swords (see Luke 16:14-15; Rom. 2:1; Rev. 12:10-11).

Destroyer

The *fourth* and final nature of the adversary is to *destroy*. Satan uses God's Law to his own advantage, working similar to an evil police officer. Using entrapment, he persuades people to sin and then penalizes them for their trespasses.

Satan is the administrator of the curses of the Law. The tempter delights in persuading people to break God's commandments because, when they do, he obtains the right to afflict them. Unlike God, who takes no pleasure in the death of the wicked, satan rejoices in their destruction (see Ps. 94:20; Ezek. 33:11; Rom. 7:5,8-11; 1 Cor. 10:10).

Chapter 10

A NEW CONCEPT

L et us now contemplate one more important concept before looking in detail at the mysterious scorpion:

> *For the preaching of the cross is to them that perish foolishness; but unto us which are saved it is the power of God* (1 Corinthians 1:18).

The power of God for healing and deliverance is in the cross of Christ. The cross is the only legitimate way to obtain God's abundant provision (see John 10:1). Proper comprehension of the cross is essential for the Church to obtain complete healing.

First, we should understand that the cross is *not* an instrument of torture for Christians. Jesus commanded His followers to take up their cross and follow Him, and truly, *"His commandments are not grievous"* (see 1 John 5:3). The perception of the cross as being a grievous burden is not what God intended.

The true meaning of the cross is expressed in Matthew 11:28, *"Come unto me, all ye that labour and are heavy laden, and I will give you rest."* The cross is an instrument of rest! As Jesus approached the cross, Luke recorded, *"When the time was come that He should be received up, He steadfastly set His face to go to Jerusalem"* (Luke 9:51). Jesus was received of God and entered into His rest through the cross. Therefore, we see the cross' foremost purpose is to provide a way for us to cease from our own works and enter into God's presence. The cross of Christ is the only instrument provided by God through which we may present ourselves to God and by which we are received and accepted of God.

Adam and his descendants were driven from the presence of God by sin. Through the cross, people reenter God's presence and are accepted by Him through Christ's sacrificial offering (see Eph. 1:5-6). In His presence is fullness of joy, comfort, peace, and everything else people may need (see Ps. 16:11). So, first, people are received by God through the cross, *and second, they receive all they need, from God, through the cross.*

> *Yet it pleased the Lord to bruise Him; He hath put Him to grief: when Thou shalt make His soul an offering for sin, He shall see His seed, He shall prolong His days, and the pleasure of the Lord shall prosper in His hand* (Isaiah 53:10).

This is not torture; this is joy! To take up your cross is to forsake the world and, through Christ, come into a living relationship with God:

> *But God forbid that I should glory, save in the cross of our Lord Jesus Christ, by whom the world is crucified unto me, and I unto the world* (Galatians 6:14).

The *world* is crucified unto each Christian through the cross of Christ. People are not to look to the world to satisfy their needs or desires. Likewise, through the cross, *they* are crucified to the world. For this reason Christians should deny any passion or longing that would draw them toward the things of the world. The *self* that Jesus said each of His followers must deny refers to these desires (see Mark 8:34; Col. 3:1-5). When people are "lifted up on the cross," they are established in a vertical relationship with God. At the same time their horizontal connection with the world is severed, or destroyed.

As we continue, we will see that God gave people their desires and called them good (see Gen. 1:27-31). God's intention was to be the One to fulfill those desires and to meet each and every one of humanity's needs. This is one of the reasons God forbade Adam from eating of the tree of the knowledge of good and evil. God was aware that it would become a substitute for the provision that He intended to supply.

So our cross is not sickness—neither is it the ministry which we perform, nor the burden of caring for our neighbor—our cross is the lifting of ourselves and our desires to God, looking to Him, through Christ, to fulfill all our needs!

> *But my God shall supply all your needs according to His riches in glory by Christ Jesus* (Philippians 4:19).

In Philippians 3:18-19, Paul uses the phrase, *"enemies of the cross,"* referring to those *"who mind earthly things."* He admonished the Colossians to, *"Set your affections on things above, not on things on the earth"* (Col. 3:2). People can only accomplish this by correcting their attitudes (values) and redirecting their desires toward the things of God.

Everything people value must be from above. Everything they esteem as worthy of their love (care and concern), worthy of their labor, or worthy of pursuing and obtaining must be from and through God. When people value anything of the world as precious or worthy of adoration and worship they endanger their relationship with God. Even esteeming something as worthy of apprehension and worry hinders communion with God (see Luke 14:26-27,33):

> *Love not the world, neither the things that are in the world. If any man love the world, the love of the Father is not in him. For all that is in the world, the lust of the flesh, and the lust of the eyes, and the pride of life, is not of the Father, but is of the world* (1 John 2:15-16).

> *Lo, this only have I found, that God hath made man upright; but they have sought out many inventions* (Ecclesiastes 7:29).

God made people morally upright, with intense longings directed toward their creator. Humanity was consecrated to God just as a bride is separated unto her husband (see Eph. 5:24-32). This separation is why God sees all devotion to the things of this world as spiritual adultery:

> *Ye adulterers and adulteresses, know ye not that the friendship of the world is enmity with God? whosoever therefore will be a friend of the world is the enemy of God* (James 4:4).

From the beginning God was to be humanity's provider, friend, and companion. God created people to worship Him just as a bride reverences her husband. People were to look to God to provide the love, pleasure, protection, and anything and everything else they needed (see Gen. 2:8-9; Heb. 12:2).

*We should understand that this does **not** mean that our fellowship with God is completely without sacrifice.* Because of the proper attitude people develop by accepting God's Word as truth, when necessary, they even find pleasure in suffering for Christ's sake (see Acts 5:40-41; Phil. 1:29):

> *And He said unto me, "My grace is sufficient for thee: for My strength is made perfect in weakness." Most gladly therefore will I rather glory in my infirmities, that the power of Christ may rest upon me. Therefore I take pleasure in infirmities, in reproaches, in necessities, in persecutions, in distresses for Christ's sake: for when I am weak, then am I strong* (2 Corinthians 12:9-10).

Many Christians really do not believe those words of Paul. With their mouths they pledge allegiance to God and His Word, but their hearts are not in agreement when it actually comes to suffering (see Matt. 15:8-9). But it is a wrong attitude toward suffering that makes it seem so unpleasant, not the experience itself. People often work in unappealing secular jobs without much thought about the discomfort because they expect payment for their troubles. Likewise, a Christian should willingly embrace the inconvenience of God's work. After all, the reward for God's work is far

greater and longer lasting than any paycheck received in this world (see
2 Cor. 4:16-18; Heb. 10:34; 1 Pet. 4:12-14):

> [Moses chose] *to suffer affliction with the people of God,*
> [rather] *than to enjoy the pleasures of sin for a season; esteem-*
> *ing the reproach of Christ greater riches than the treasures in*
> *Egypt: for he had respect unto the recompense of the reward*
> (Hebrews 11:25-26).

God said those who suffer with Him would also rule with Him (see
2 Tim. 2:12). Christians should emulate Paul. He said:

> *I count all things but loss for the excellency of the knowledge of*
> *Christ Jesus my Lord... That I may know Him, and the power*
> *of His resurrection, and the fellowship of His sufferings, being*
> *made conformable unto His death* (Philippians 3:8,10).

In summary, as Christians, our cross is the lifting of ourselves and our
desires to God, looking to God, through Christ, to fulfill all our needs.
Therefore, knowing the faithfulness of God, we *"rejoice in* [our] *sufferings...*
and fill up that which is behind of the afflictions of Christ in [our] *flesh for His*
body's sake, which is the church" (Col. 1:24).

The Motions of Sin

Let us now look at the scorpion in detail, examining each sin sepa-
rately. Keep in mind that when a frog is dissected in a biology laboratory,
it is killed to anatomize it. In the same way, we must separate and dissect
each sin before we can understand it. For a frog to demonstrate life, appetite, and motion, it must be intact, using muscle, nerve, blood, and bone
together. So it is with iniquity. People's attitudes, desires, and actions inter-
act with each other to produce the actual motions of sin. Nevertheless,
for the sake of understanding, we will separate and analyze each specific
aspect of sin (see Rom. 7:5).

As we carefully examine the Scriptures in the next chapters, keep in mind that *a scorpion represents the sin nature of humanity's flesh and carnal mind.* The eight eyes of the scorpion correspond to the eight desires of humanity's flesh and carnal mind, and the scorpion's legs represent the eight roots of sin, or attitudes.

To overcome the natural tendency to sin people have to cut off the scorpion's legs. The axe (the cross of Christ) must be used on the root attitudes that are incorrectly held in the conscious mind. The natural desires are then redirected from the things of the world to the things of God.

> *But God forbid that I should glory, save in the cross of our Lord Jesus Christ, by whom the world is crucified unto me, and I unto the world* (Galatians 6:14).

> *Behold, I give unto you power to tread on serpents and scorpions, and over all the power of the enemy* (Luke 10:19).

Chapter 11

ENEMIES OF THE CROSS

*But the fearful, and unbelieving, and the abominable, and murderers, and whoremongers, and sorcerers, and **idolaters**, and all liars, shall have their part in the lake which burneth with fire and brimstone: which is the second death* (Revelation 21:8).

The logic of beginning our detailed analysis of the scorpion with the sin category of *idolatry* is revealed when we consider the often quoted words of Paul, *"The love of money is the root of all evil"* (1 Tim. 6:10). This taproot of iniquity permeates all sin, but it is *the* root of covetousness, which is idolatry. Paul also said, *"They that will be rich fall into temptation and a snare, and into many foolish and hurtful lusts, which drown men in destruction and perdition"* (1 Tim. 6:9; see also Col. 3:5).

Certainly, the love of money has lured many people, *"into temptation and a snare, and into many foolish and hurtful lusts,"* but Paul's statement, *"the love of money"* encompasses a much broader application than money alone (see 1 Tim. 6:9). Before we can fully comprehend and appreciate what Paul actually meant, the wording he used must be closely examined.

The Greek phrase *phil-arguria*, from which the expression "love of money" is derived, specifically refers to silver. A more exact translation of *phil-arguria* is "fondness for silver." The root word *argos*, from which *arguria* is derived means "shining." Thus, fondness for that which *shines*, whether literally or figuratively, is what actually causes the covetous desires of the flesh and carnal mind. This interpretation can be both verified and understood by examining the scriptural record of Adam and Eve's first sin (see Gen. 2:9, 3:1-6).

Since this root is present in all evil, we should be able to find this fatal attraction in the very first sin in the Garden of Eden:

> *And when the woman saw that the tree* [of knowledge of good and evil] *was good for food, and that it was pleasant to the eyes, and a tree to be desired to make one wise, she took of the fruit thereof, and did eat, and gave also unto her husband with her and he did eat* (Genesis 3:6).

Obviously, there was no money or silver growing on the tree that caused Eve's fall. *This tree's attraction came directly from its fruit—knowledge.* It was also the desire for knowledge, both to acquire and display it, that Paul observed in the city of Athens. This city was *wholly* given to idolatry.

> *Now while Paul waited… his spirit was stirred in him, when he saw the city wholly given to idolatry… (For all the Athenians and strangers which were there spent their time in nothing else, but either to tell, or to hear some new thing)* (Acts 17:16,21).

God uses the term *knowledge* in a much deeper sense than just intellectual awareness. Adam *knew* Eve and she conceived (see Gen. 4:1). Paul spoke of forsaking all for the excellency of the *knowledge* of Christ Jesus (see Phil. 3:8). The Greek word used here means experiential knowledge, or knowledge based on experience. This knowledge is far more intimate and complete than just intellectual knowledge.

The impulsive desire to *know* the tree's fruit, admire it, handle it, taste it, and possess it in the most intimate way possible drew Eve into disobedience. To the eye it was pleasant to look at, to the flesh it was enjoyable to eat, and for the mind it would make one wise—like God. In each case, it was good! Yet God said that it was poisonous, that it would destroy anyone who ate of its fruit!

It is this desire to *know* good (as the flesh esteems good) and evil (that which is forbidden) that lies at the root of all sin. But it is the *"good"* knowledge that especially deceives people. The eye desires knowledge—to see and examine that which it has not seen before. The ambition of the mind is to know those things that it has not known before. The flesh desires to experience all that its senses are capable of experiencing in the most intimate and experiential way possible.

We should realize that the flesh has no factual consciousness of evil. If it feels comfortable, looks good, sounds enjoyable, smells pleasant, or is pleasing to the taste, then it *is* good, as far as the flesh is concerned. This can be seen in the modern slogan, *"If it feels good, do it."* But Paul said there is nothing good in the flesh (see Rom. 7:18).

Likewise, the natural curiosity of the carnal mind loves intimate knowledge of all kinds. Curiosity, with the tantalizing lure of hidden secrets, draws people into such things as mysterious, fraternal lodges, and sometimes even the occult. Gossip, tragedies, and triumphs are also juicy feasts for the carnal mind.

The human spirit, alone, has true consciousness of good and evil. It is the mind of the spirit (conscience) that satan must reason with and placate before he can seduce people into sin. Delilah caused Samson to sleep on her knees as she enticed him with her charms (see Judg. 16:19). Likewise, satan lulls his intended victims' conscience to sleep so they will submit to his lies and reasoning. Once the conscience is calmed and subdued, satan draws people into sin through the passions of the flesh and carnal mind (see Eph. 2:2-3; James 1:14-15).

It is this ever-present passion for the knowledge of that which shines that Paul referred to as the root of all evil. Silver tarnishes quickly; likewise, the excitement of owning a new car or the initial thrill of obtaining fine jewelry soon fades. Even the honor of a new promotion quickly becomes ordinary.

People must constantly be reaching for something new, something different, something sparkling, something that causes their faces to shine with pride and happiness in order to stay satisfied. Even when they get what they are coveting, their thirst is quenched only for a little while; then they thirst again (see Prov. 27:20; Eccl. 8:1; John 4:13).

People cannot, for long, appease their ever-present, never-satisfied lusts. Unless they are vigilant and constantly polish the old, they will become fascinated and captivated by the new. Marriages fall apart as partners covet their neighbors' spouses. The ones they have, they know—the ones across the street are a mystery—a mystery they lust to solve in the most intimate way possible. As Jude 7 says, they quickly become dissatisfied and find themselves, *"going after strange flesh."*

The attitude that worldly, intimate knowledge is good, along with the resultant fondness for knowledge this opinion propagates, is the taproot of all evil. This inordinate lust, symbolized by silver's shine, is the main root that the axe must sever if people are to live free from sin.

Theologians commonly teach that silver is the biblical symbol for *redemption.* And indeed, the knowledge of God, through our Lord Jesus Christ, *is* redemption (see John 17:3). But the error of this teaching is in using the symbol itself for redemption and not the *knowledge* that brings redemption. Proverbs 2:3-5 reveals the proper use of silver as a symbol:

> *Yea, if thou criest after **knowledge**, and liftest up thy voice for understanding; if thou seekest her **as silver**, and searchest for her as for hid treasures; then shalt thou understand the fear of the Lord, and find the knowledge of God.*

Looking again at the first sin, we can distinguish three basic types of lusts—the lust of the flesh (passion for sensuous pleasure), the lust of the eye (appreciation for that which is attractive), and the pride of life (the desire to be wise). *These three categories of lust provide the fertile soil from which we grow all sin and bring it to maturity* (see 1 John 2:16).

The root brings forth the branch; the branch brings forth the fruit. People are made of earth and bear the image, or attributes, of the earthy. This is the reason people are preoccupied with carnal ambitions and are subject to the passions and lusts of the earth (see 1 Cor. 15:47-48; Rom. 8:20).

Satan did not have to produce a desire for food, beauty, or wisdom in Eve. All he had to do was activate and direct her natural appetite to focus upon those things that were forbidden.

The *eye* of the scorpion within her was her natural desire for wisdom. The motivating force, or *leg*, of the creature was her instinctive love for intimate knowledge. The *sting* was her sin, producing death. By directing her desires toward forbidden fruit, satan used the inherent nature of the scorpion within Eve's flesh to draw her into his evil snare (see James 1:14-15).

Like Eve, all people have the desire for wisdom. Like all eight of people's basic needs, or lusts, this longing is not evil within itself (see Tit. 1:15). It is with what and by whom people satisfy this craving that determines whether their deeds are considered good or evil.

God instructs His children to seek wisdom! Proverbs teaches that *"Wisdom is the principal thing; therefore get wisdom..."* (Prov. 4:7), but Paul gives further instruction in Romans 16:19, *"...I would have you wise unto that which is good, and simple concerning evil."*

Wisdom is the ability to acquire and use knowledge properly (see Prov. 8:12, 15:2,7). The wisdom from above compares spiritual things with spiritual. The world's wisdom compares natural things with natural. People's heart attitudes determine which type of knowledge they seek after (see 1 Cor. 2:13).

God created people with both the desire and the need for wisdom. God's original intention was to satisfy humanity's hunger with the knowledge of Himself (see Matt. 6:33). Satan has taken advantage of people's inherent love for wisdom and has promoted natural knowledge as a legitimate substitute to fulfill people's spiritual needs.

Jesus said that people will continue to thirst as long as they keep trying to satisfy spiritual needs with natural substances (see John 4:13-14). Only the experiential knowledge of God can fill the void that is in their hearts. The spirit's hunger cannot be satisfied with this world's goods.

Flesh lusts for flesh; spirit longs for Spirit (see Ps. 42:7). The earthy correlates to the earth, and the heavenly correlates to the Lord from Heaven. Only by feeding the spirit with spiritual food (the Word of God) and drinking spiritual drink (the Spirit of God), can the soul be satisfied (see John 1:14, 6:51; 1 Cor. 10:3-4).

We now come to the *branch,* or motions of sin, that work in people's members (see Rom. 7:5). As we have seen, people are drawn toward the world through their lusts and ambitions. When they hold mistaken attitudes in their hearts about the world, they are motivated to satisfy their lusts in foreseeable ways. Their actions are quite predictable.

Acts 17:16-21 gives a very important insight into the motions of the sin of idolatry. Paul *"saw the city* [of Athens] *wholly given to idolatry"* (Acts 17:16). All the information given in this passage of Scripture is a manifestation of this sin. Luke recorded, *"For all the Athenians...spent their time in nothing else, but either to tell, or to hear some new thing"* (Acts 17:21).

We have seen the desire to obtain knowledge is a natural desire of the flesh. To satisfy this lust through new experiences is a normal aspect of idolatry, but here the Bible reveals people wanting to *tell* something new!

By obtaining knowledge and displaying it, people show the world around them their wisdom, thereby receiving envy, or worship, from their peers. The itch to exhibit knowledge is a product of an antichrist spirit. The antichrist spirit displaces the human spirit, setting itself up in God's temple to obtain the worship that belongs to God (see 1 Cor. 3:16; 1 John 2:15-18). Covetousness is idolatry, even when people covet the envy and admiration of their neighbors (see Col. 3:5).

When people obtain something, tangible or intangible, and display it to gain the envy (worship) of others, it is antichrist—both against, and in place of, Christ. *Worship belongs to God, alone.*

Demonstrated knowledge paraded before the world puffs people up (see 1 Cor. 8:1). The Scriptures prophesy that in the latter part of this age the antichrist spirit will be personified in *"the man of sin."* He will boast both to himself and to the world that he is god (see 2 Thess. 2:3-4). That is then, but John said, *"...Even now are there many antichrists..."* (1 John 2:18).

The antichrist spirit is an enemy of the cross. It is only when people are off the cross, looking to the world for the fulfillment of their needs, that satan can fulfill his wicked lusts. For this reason, he not only has to war against the Spirit of God (anointing), but he must destroy the cross itself before he can effectively combat the power of God (see 1 Cor. 1:18).

Paul said that when he was weak, God was strong (see 2 Cor. 12:10). Who is as impotent as those nailed to their crosses? When people are dead to the world, they are weak in relationship to the world. At the same time, they are alive to God and mighty through their relationship with Him. Their life is truly, *"sown in weakness* [but] *raised in power"* (1 Cor. 15:43).

The ultimate goal of the antichrist spirit is to deceive people into *self worship,* their own belly becoming their God (see Phil. 3:19). This is apparent in their desire to display worldly wisdom. This was Eve's downfall. Satan told her, *"Ye shall be* [known] *as gods, knowing good and evil"* (Gen. 3:5).

Status Symbols

Although people display their (worldly) wisdom many different ways, one popular method is with a *status symbol.* A status symbol may be the prettiest car or the most powerful gun, the most expensive jewelry or the largest diamond, the finest house or the most distinguished position, or even the latest news or the juiciest gossip. Even a younger wife (or mistress) or a more handsome or wealthy husband are coveted by some as means to obtain worship! Anything will do as long as it exalts people above their peers.

We can understand status symbols further by recognizing them as extensions and magnifications of people's *self.* A vain teenager, whose self-image is one of power, may try to exhibit this image through a powerful truck or car. A distinguished man drives a prestigious automobile (whether in size or cost) to display his self-perceived greatness. Something as simple as smoking a pipe or cigar is another way some attempt to project the image of having superior wisdom.

God wars against this prideful display of worldly wisdom. He pulls down those glorifying themselves and exalts those who lift their hearts to Him, humbling themselves before the world (see John 7:18; Acts 12:21-23). The humble are not competing with God and one another for worship; rather they are the true worshipers of God (see Luke 18:10-14; James 4:5-6).

The Bible teaches that idolatry is covetousness and covetousness is idolatry. Covetous people do not inherit the Kingdom of God (see 1 Cor. 6:9-10; Col. 3:5). This is startling when we learn the true meaning of the Greek word translated "covetousness"—*to have, to hold, and to desire more!* Can today's Christians claim innocence? Yet who has even considered himself or herself as a worshiper of idols?

A very common saying today is, *"The next thing I am going to buy is...."* Covetousness is the only thing we can call this. Many of today's Christians have disregarded and ignored the scriptural admonition, *"Set your affections on things above, **not** on things on the earth"* (Col. 3:2).

Jesus said that if His followers would seek first the Kingdom of God and His righteousness, then God would provide all their needs (see Matt. 6:33). More than that, the Bible even says that He will provide the good things they desire (see Ps. 37:4).

If Christians are seeking His will and rule and not their own, they are content in whatever state they are in (see Phil. 4:11): *"Great peace have they which love thy law* [rule] *and nothing shall offend them... [neither] ...death, nor life, nor angels, nor principalities, nor powers, nor things present, nor things to come... nor any other creature..."* (Ps. 119:165; Rom. 8:38-39; see also Matt. 11:6). But, if people covet worldly possessions, sooner or later they will be offended by the loss of their idols.

When Jacob's wife, Rachel, stole her father Laban's images, he was very angry. Laban credited his family idols, or gods, with blessing him with success. The loss of his graven images caused him to fear losing everything they represented to him (see Gen. 31:30-36). Many Christians, too, are offended when they lose their worldly possessions and the relationships which they hold dear.

Because of this Paul warned covetous people that sorrow awaits them. Grief is the portion allotted to everyone who pursues the natural desire to be rich (see 1 Tim. 6:9-10). Satan labors to impart an attitude that people can obtain happiness through intimate knowledge of the world. This is idolatry. God assures all people that *idolatry brings grief.*

Another popular form of idolatry is hero worship. If people worship people, whether they worship their friends, family, heroes, or movie stars, there is always an open door for offence or grief to enter when their idol fails or dies.

Every person will one day be separated from all material things. *"For we brought nothing into this world, and it is certain we can carry nothing out"* (1 Tim. 6:7). For this reason, let everyone obey God and, *"set your affections on things above, not on things on this earth"* (Col. 3:2). Christians, in learning to correct wrong attitudes about their relationships with God and the world, should be careful to distinguish between attitudes and actions. Luke 12:15 warns, *"Take heed, and beware of covetousness: for a man's life consisteth not in the abundance of the things which he possesseth."*

This statement is given to correct wrong attitudes, not to segregate people from material things altogether (see 1 Cor. 7:29-31). For instance, the Bible says, *"...If riches increase, set not your heart upon them"* (Ps. 62:10). It does not say to refuse them or even necessarily to give them away, but it does warn everyone that *"Riches certainly make themselves wings; they fly away"* (Prov. 23:5).

When people's hearts are set on riches, if they lose their wealth, or even the hope of becoming wealthy, they will become upset and open to grief through this loss. Their misfortune offends them (see Prov. 13:12;

Mark 10:21-23). A Christian's attitude toward gain should be like Job's: *"...The Lord gave, and the Lord hath taken away; blessed be the name of the Lord"* (Job 1:21). Christians should simply wave good-bye to the departed wealth and *"press toward the mark for the prize...* [of the]... *true riches"* (see Phil. 3:7-14; Luke 16:11).

When people's hearts are filled with *"the treasures of wisdom and knowledge"* (Col. 2:3), they have eternal wealth. When people have *"all riches of the full assurance of understanding...which shall never be taken away"* (Col. 2:2; Luke 10:42) then, indeed, they have true riches!

Christians should also differentiate between the motives which are behind their actions. Nearly everyone has to work to obtain worldly goods, but the motive of the heart is all important. Some people labor selfishly for personal gain; others labor *"to have to give to him that needeth"* (Eph. 4:28). It is not always what we do, but what makes us do what we do, that counts with God.

Principality (Rule)

We have seen that a spirit of *error* works to put incorrect attitudes (values) toward the world into people's minds (see 1 John 4:5-6). If, through the influence of this evil spirit, people accept the idea that life is in the abundance of the things they own, their minds and emotions are receptive to the spirit of antichrist. Jesus said people could not worship God and mammon. They would hold to the one and hate (be offended by) the other (see Matt. 6:24).

Power (Authority)

The spirit of *antichrist* is the spirit that persuades people to replace God in their hearts and lives with the things of the world (see 1 John 2:15-18). These substitutes can be people, material possessions, or even spiritual things other than God, such as the occult.

If people worship anything or anyone other than God, it is *anti*-Christ, that is, something that replaces Christ. The Greek prefix translated "anti" means "in place of." To participate in wrong worship is to yield their members to this unclean spirit.

Might

As Paul warned, the desire for riches and other worldly things causes men to:

> *...Fall into temptation and a snare, and into many foolish and hurtful lusts, which drown men in destruction and perdition.... they have erred from the faith, and pierced themselves through with many sorrows* (1 Timothy 6:9-10).

Those who are drowning are filled with anguish and despair.

It is obvious that once people are misled by the spirit of error and become subject to an antichrist spirit's authority, the powerful spirit of **heaviness** (sorrow, grief, etc.) soon has an open door into their hearts. This demon strives to bring people into depression and despondency (see Isa. 61:3). When people become offended in their grief over their failures, misfortunes, and disappointments, they are subject to the spirit of heaviness (see Prov. 13:12; Mark 10:21-22; Luke 16:13).

They forget God in their "pursuit of happiness" and, even worse, become competitors with Him. Then, as Adam and Eve were forced to leave the Garden of Eden by the presence of God, they are also rejected by their Creator.

> *And even as they did not like to retain God in their knowledge, God* [rejected them and] *gave them over to a reprobate mind, to do those things which are not convenient* (Romans 1:28).

Dominion (Mastery)

Being rejected, they are subject to a spirit of **rejection**. Paul prophesied that in the last days people would be *"without natural affection"* (1 Tim. 3:3). The Greek phrase translated here means, *"hard hearted toward one's own kindred."* Through the influence of this spirit, people become callous and inhuman in their feelings toward those they should naturally love (see 1 Tim. 3:1-3, 4:1-2; Eph. 4:19). God rejected His children because He was offended by their sin. Human parents reject their children because of the sin that is in their own hearts (see Rom. 2:1).

Some parents, in their attempts to satisfy their fleshly lust and carnal ambitions, neglect, ignore, deprive, or even abuse their own children. When children are rejected, for whatever reason, they tend to retaliate. One way is to simply reject those who have rejected them (which is usually perceived as rebellion). Once they yield to the spirit of rejection, they become a servant of rejection through the Law of Dominion.

God is the Father of all people. The spirit of rejection works to harden people's hearts toward all of their kin, including their Heavenly Father. Proverbs 19:3 says, *"The foolishness of man perverts his way: and his heart fretteth against the Lord."* When events happen to people that bring defeat or frustration, they may direct thoughts toward God like, *"Why did You let this happen to me?"* Or, if instead they blame another person for their calamity, they may rage, *"This wouldn't have happened if you would have listened to me!"* or, *"If it weren't for you..."* These types of accusations have been with us from the beginning: Adam accused God and Eve for his error instead of acknowledging his sin as his own mistake (see Gen. 3:12).

When a society rejects its own children, seeing them as a burden because of their love for the world, they sin. As wives spurn their husbands and husbands idolize other women, rejecting their wives in the process, the *sin of idolatry* reaches its fullness.

When a nation has fallen into degradation and its citizens are devoted to sin, they invoke God's wrath. Once they replace God in their hearts with the things of the world, they bring God's wrath and judgment down upon themselves (see Rom. 1:18; Col. 3:5-6).

In summary, we have seen how the *error* of *idolizing* anything, or anyone, other than God, is *antichrist*. This spirit brings people into *grief*, sorrow, and *hard-heartedness* toward God and others.

As people become hardened through the deceitfulness of sin, they are *rejected* by God (see Heb. 3:11-13). Rejected, they are without hope (depression) and are separated from God's abundant provision (see Gen. 3:23-24; Prov. 13:12; Eph. 2:12). When they are separated from God, instead of repenting, they often try, horizontally, to fill their souls' hunger and thirst with fleshly relationships and material possessions—the very things that caused their sad condition in the first place.

As we continue this study, remember that each dominion spirit works to open people's hearts to the next principality. It is like the water-wheel at a country gristmill; as each bucket fills with water, its weight rotates the wheel to bring the next bucket into the path of the waterfall, and it in turn fills to continue the relentless process. This motion is indicated by the curved arrow on the *Wheel of Nature* in the illustration immediately preceding each of the chapters on the eight categories of sin. We will examine, in depth, the part that the dominion spirit of rejection plays in causing the Wheel of Nature to revolve in the next chapter.

Sin—Idolatry

Lust (Eye)—Love of Wisdom
Root (Leg)—Love of Money (or Knowledge)
Branch (Motion)—Covetousness

Spirits

Principality (Rule)—Error
Power (Authority)—Antichrist
Might (Miracle Power)—Heaviness
Dominion (Mastery)—Rejection

Fruits

Without natural affections; Grief; Sorrow;
Loneliness; Selfishness; etc.

Some Common Sins in this Category

Theft; Fraud; Gambling; Cheating; Over indebtedness;
Evil imaginations; Child neglect

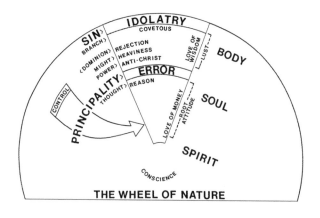

THE WHEEL OF NATURE

Chapter 12

SINNERS AGAINST THEMSELVES

But the fearful, and unbelieving, and the abominable, and murderers, and whoremongers [fornicators], *and sorcerers, and idolaters, and all liars, shall have their part in the lake which burneth with fire and brimstone...* (Revelation 21:8).

*F*ornication is to the body as idolatry is to the mind. The Word of God charges all people, *"Flee from idolatry"* (1 Cor. 10:14). Likewise, they are warned to flee from fornication:

Flee fornication. Every sin that a man [commits] *is without the body; but he that committeth fornication sinneth against his own body* (1 Corinthians 6:18).

In Acts 15:20, James wrote to the churches and told them they should *"abstain from pollutions of idols, and from fornication...."* He then continued with, *"from which if ye keep yourselves, ye shall do well"* (Acts 15:29).

If people keep their minds and bodies in obedience to God in these matters, there is no room for sin. Fondness for intimate knowledge of the things of the world is the root of *all* evil; therefore, people leave little room for sin if their thirst for knowledge is filled from above. The thirst of both humanity's flesh and carnal mind can only be quenched by heeding the one who is perfect in knowledge—God (see Prov. 2:3-5; John 4:13-14).

The spirit of this world must put an incorrect attitude into people's minds about themselves before he can seduce them into selling themselves cheaply. As long as they know and acknowledge the truth about themselves, the truth defends them against satan's deception. But, by penetrating this defense and causing men to receive wrong attitudes in their minds about themselves and one another, satan leads them into slavery. The price he pays people for their souls is the pleasures of sin (see Isa. 50:1, 52:3). To understand the way he accomplishes this purchase, we need to look more closely at the spirit of rejection.

Remember that rejection is a product of idolatry. When people are rejected by others, they are given a message that they *are* rejects. When this message is believed, they feel inferior to others. This results in the development of a lower self-image than they should have.

Without a proper self-image, people will sell themselves cheaply— even for something as cheap and evanescent as the fleeting pleasures of sin. This is true whether they commit actual fleshly fornication or adultery or the spiritual adultery of being friends with the world. When people have improper self-image, they will usually fall into sin unless God intervenes (see James 4:4).

When people view themselves as inferior or lower than others, a need to climb higher becomes activated within them. This compelling desire to ascend higher, or the desire to conquer, is the "eye" of the scorpion within man.

As with all eight of the lusts, this desire remains dormant, or unfulfilled, unless it is motivated to gratification. The motivating "leg" of the scorpion is an improper, low self-image with its resultant improper self-esteem.

An example of the competitive ambition induced by rejection can be seen in the biblical story of Jephthah and his brethren. Jephthah was the illegitimate son of a harlot. Because he was illegitimate, his siblings drove him out of their home to keep him from sharing in their inheritance. Being shamed, rejected, and forced out of his home produced an aggressive drive within him, motivating him to become *"a mighty man of valor"* (see Judg. 11:1-3).

When Israel needed a deliverer, they turned to this rejection-made man. Jephthah's bargaining response to his brethren's request for help reveals his heart, *"If ye bring me home again to fight against the children of Ammon, and the Lord deliver them before me, shall I be your head"* (Judg. 11:9).

Beside the desire to conquer, another of the devastating effects of rejection is revealed in this story. In his desire to win pre-eminence over his brethren Jephthah made a foolish vow which resulted in the sacrifice of his daughter (see Judg. 11:30-31;34-39). No sacrifice was too great to promise, or surrender, if he could become the head of Israel.

As we discussed in the last chapter, and as we can see from this story, *rejection hardens people's hearts toward their own kindred.* As rejected people strive to ascend higher in their own self-image and self-esteem, they often sacrifice their family in the process.

Fathers, hardening their hearts to their loved one's hurts and needs, leave their wives and children. In the pursuit of other women, prominent positions in corporations, or other selfish quests, they ignore the damage they are doing to those whom they are supposed to love. Mothers are also drawn into the snare of sin, sometimes deserting their own children as they attempt to fill their inner need for acceptance and love (see Hos. 2:2-5; John 4:16-18).

Another good example of the results of rejection is the life of Samson. Samson's infamous weakness for women and his invincible strength were both motivated by rejection. The form of rejection suffered by Samson is the most complex and perplexing of all. He was a smothered child.

Samson's mother was barren for many years. When her only child finally arrived, he was long coveted after. As a result, it was perfectly normal for Samson's parents to indulge his every whim (see Judg. 13:2-3, 14:1-3).

This was reflected in the selfish and self-indulging lifestyle he lived. Unlike Samuel, who was born under similar circumstances, but was raised in a life of service, Samson never did anything without a self-centered, selfish motive (see Judg. 15:1-8, 16:1-3,28).

Sometimes parents smother their children because of fear for their safety or even out of fear that their children may turn out like they did. Restricting them from a normal social life, driving them to achieve, and many other similar actions, all may result in their offspring feeling rejected.

Smothered children are rejected in their identity. It is the struggle to be unique, to be an individual, that brings forth a competitive urge or an obsession to conquer. For example, Samson undoubtedly received a certain amount of rejection from his friends when he was a child. The religious vow of asceticism that he was raised under set him apart from his peers. His uncut hair and the fact that he was severely restricted in social activities opened his heart to rejection.

Self-imposed regulations and restraints, which the Scripture calls *"will worship,"* is religious legalism (see Col. 2:20-23). Religion, when imposed on children, often produces the opposite affect of that which is intended. In their attempts to raise their children correctly, parents confine them to make them pure. Instead, the children turn to the world to find the acceptance and love they could not find in the religious system in which they were raised.

The increase of such sins as date rape, child molestation, homosexuality, and general promiscuity are all products of an idolatrous (religious, but not godly) society (see Acts 17:22). A materialistic society invariably rejects its own children.

Rejection takes many forms. Regardless of the reason or way that rejection is received, it invariably destroys people's self-image and, thereby, their self-esteem. Infidelity in marriage often occurs as rejected partners strive to climb higher in their own self-image and self-esteem. *Rejected people feel unloved and unwanted.* To satisfy the hunger and to fill the empty void in their hearts, they reach out to others for the acceptance they need. Striving to grasp and obtain a healthy self-respect through the acceptance of others often produces unfaithfulness and immorality.

This occurs whether the rejection is deeply ingrained in people's personalities from childhood or from their present marriage or a previously failed marriage. Jesus said, *"Whosoever shall put away his wife...causes her to commit adultery"* (Matt. 5:32). For a husband to put away (reject) his wife destroys her self-image. Rejection makes her perceive herself as a reject, marring her self-image and diminishing her self-respect. This is also true concerning men when they are rejected by their wives.

The significance of proper self-image and the resultant healthy self-esteem cannot be overemphasized. Much of the spiritual health of a society rests upon this foundational principle.

The Bond of Marriage

Even the bond of the marriage relationship is formed and maintained through the proper perception of self and spouse. In the beginning God formed Adam, the first man. From this man He brought forth Eve and presented her to Adam. In doing this, God gave humanity the ordinance of marriage. God performed the first marriage and fashioned the first family, the basic building block of society (see Gen. 2:22-25; Mark 10:6-9).

The bond of marriage is emotional attraction. God set the precedent for this bond while man was still in the garden. This attachment is formed by positional relationship. Adam, when presented with his wife said, *"Therefore shall a man leave his father and mother* [becoming an authority within himself], *and shall cleave unto his wife..."* (Gen. 2:24). And to the woman God said, *"...thy desire shall be to thy husband, and he shall rule over thee"* (Gen. 3:16).

The truth that the emotional bond is formed by the man and woman each being in their proper place in their relationship is easily illustrated. We can see this bond being formed by looking at the reason so many men become emotionally entangled with their secretaries or other female employees.

In a typical example, we notice that the female employee depends upon her employer for support, approval, correction, and direction. *In short, she must look up to him, exalt him, reverence him, and obey him.* As she walks in true obedience, her boss is delighted by her responsive attention. The effect of her obedience is to form an emotional attraction in him toward her.

At home, if his wife is not submissive and loving, he begins to lose the passionate bond he had formed with his "Eve" in the beginning of his relationship with her. As he is fondly drawn toward his secretary or other female employee and begins to cleave to her, she responds to his warmth and affection.

We love God because He first loved us (see 1 John 4:19); likewise, the woman returns her employer's affectionate gestures, words, gifts, and similar acts of kindness. *When we are obedient to God, we are emotionally drawn to Him.* When a woman is subordinate and obedient to a kind man, she is drawn to him in her emotions. *Being submissive, she draws emotional affection from him, which he equates with love.* When she is loved, she responds with passionate feelings that she also regards as love. This often results in an affair that destroys one or both of their marriages. That which begins so innocently and seems so natural and beautiful becomes a love trap which ensnares them and draws them into sin.

Many times this cycle is repeated when the female employee marries her employer. Failing to maintain the submissive relationship she walked in as an employee, she participates in setting the stage for the breakup of her own marriage also.

When a wife reverences her husband and the husband loves his wife as God intended (see Eph. 5:33 AMP), the marriage bond is secure and the normal emotional and sexual needs of both are provided for in the God-given and God-ordained ordinance of marriage (see Gen. 24:67; 1 Cor. 7:2-5).

The Marriage Bed Undefiled

We should not overlook the significance of Genesis 2:25: *"And they were both naked, the man and his wife, and were not ashamed."* There is no shame or guilt in the normal sexual relationship within the confines of marriage (see Heb. 13:4).

This is not to imply, as some have stated, that all sexual activity between married partners is without sin. Some hold that mutual consent is the only criterion for judging sexual activity, regardless of how abnormal it is. First Thessalonians 4:4-5 specifically states that the sexual relationship is to be *"in sanctification and honor; not in the lust of concupiscence* [a longing, especially for what is forbidden]."

When either of the marriage partners perceives something in their sexual relationship as unacceptable and his or her conscience is bothered by that activity, he or she should abstain from whatever condemns the conscience. Paul said it was necessary to keep the conscience void of offense toward God and man (see Acts 24:16). *The partner who is not convicted in conscience is required by the Word of God to submit to the weaker conscience of the other* (see 1 Cor. 8:12).

To ignore this puts a strain on the relationship that in many cases will endanger the marriage. When one partner feels condemned, it is the responsibility of the other partner to abstain until both can agree upon what is acceptable and what is not.

When the husband walks in love toward his wife, he will not humble her to submit to any sexual desire that he has that her conscience will not agree with. *Walking in submission to her husband does not require the wife to disobey the higher authority of her conscience* (see Rom. 13:1). Likewise, the husband is responsible to keep both his conscience and the marriage bed undefiled (see Heb. 13:4).

Obedience to God comes first. The Word of God and the conscience are higher in authority than the husband. This should be obvious because it is through the Word of God that the husband obtains his position of authority in the family (see Gen. 3:16; 1 Cor. 11:3).

Homosexuality

Another manifestation of the sin of fornication is homosexuality. This, too, is caused by an improper self-image. If people have been severely rejected and have a very low self-image, they will look up to, or reverence, others of the same sex. Feeling subordinate instead of equal to others of the same sex can draw people into a homosexual, instead of a normal heterosexual, relationship. This can happen to males and females alike.

A nation invariably falls into homosexuality when its society rejects its own children for convenience and material possessions. The rejected children (those who are fortunate enough to escape abortion) develop a poor self-image. Because they feel inferior, they esteem others of their own sex as being superior to themselves. Because they are subordinate in their own minds, immoral and inordinate sensations and affections develop within their minds and emotions.

To understand the motions of homosexuality further, study Sodom, the very epitome of this sin. Although Sodom has long been equated with homosexuality, *the sin of idolatry was Sodom's first sin.* Homosexuality was the result of Sodom's idolatry.

> *Behold, this was the iniquity of thy sister Sodom, pride, fullness of bread, and abundance of idleness was in her and in her daughters, neither did she strengthen the hand of the poor and needy* [selfishness]. *And they were haughty, and committed abomination before me; therefore I took them away as I saw good* (Ezekiel 16:49-50).

This Scripture reveals that a selfish, materialistic lifestyle and a prideful flaunting of her self-perceived superiority (idolatry) preceded Sodom's fall into homosexuality. Exalting herself led to her downfall. It is important to see the spiritual legacy of Sodom:

Thou art thy mother's daughter, that loatheth [rejected] *her husband and her children; and thou art the sister of thy sister, which loathed* [rejected] *their husbands and their children...* (Ezekiel 16:45).

One can see, then, that rejection, which is the result of idolatry, caused Sodom's fall into homosexuality. Paul said they *"became vain in their imaginations"* and refused to *"retain God in their knowledge,...professing themselves to be wise, they became fools"* (Rom. 1:21,28).

Rejection

As we have seen, rejection can be received or administered many different ways. Parents too busy fulfilling their own needs or selfish desires to give their children the love and acceptance they need is but one of many ways that children can receive a spirit of rejection. Rejection may also be encountered through several other channels.

The death of a parent can cause enormous trauma in a young child heart. Unable to understand death, the little one receives lasting wounds that only God can heal. Rejection experienced by children whose parents die is as genuine as any other. It is the same as the rejection experienced when a parent deserts the family or when parents divorce.

Parents also open their children's hearts to rejection by ignoring them, taunting and mocking them, scornfully ridiculing them, screaming insults and curses at them, or physically abusing them. Incest or sexual molestation is another form of rejection. When children are treated as sex objects instead of as people, they view themselves as inferior and less than what God made them to be.

Partiality shown by parents among their children, or even toward others outside the family, causes rejection. Partiality gives the less favored children the subtle message that they are different and not accepted as the others are.

Fathers who work on jobs away from home, such as military service, traveling sales, or offshore oil drilling are another common source of rejection. A mother's absence while working outside the home can also cause emotional wounds and open children to a spirit of rejection.

Friends can also be a source of rejection. They can leave scars in children's hearts by dying, moving away, or just shunning them in favor of someone else.

Although rejection is by far the most common cause of an inappropriate self-image, there are other reasons. The order of birth gives people certain natural advantages or disadvantages. An older brother or sister goes places and becomes involved in activities that the younger children cannot partake of. The younger siblings must stay home until they are older. Younger children feel rejected when they are not allowed to partake of their older siblings activities. Physical size, gender, athletic ability, natural talents, beauty, or intelligence can also play a very significant role in how people view themselves.

When people are rejected or for other reasons are overcome with feelings of insignificance or inferiority, they usually receive a spirit of rejection. *"...For of whom a man is overcome, of the same is he brought in bondage"* (2 Pet. 2:19). This aspect of the Law of Dominion has far-reaching implications.

When children are sexually molested, they receive the same evil spirits the molester has! Child molesters have a spirit of sexual lust (whoredoms) and a spirit of guilt. As a result, the violated children also receive a spirit of whoredoms and a spirit of guilt, in addition to a spirit of rejection.

Similarly, rapists normally have the unclean spirits of hatred, sexual lust (whoredoms), and guilt. Their victims receive these same evil spirits— hatred, whoredoms, and guilt, plus rejection. When people are overcome by evil, they receive whatever unclean spirits their oppressors have that compelled them to do wrong.

A demon's function is to work his nature both through and upon the people he inhabits. People with a spirit of rejection will reject others and, likewise, will fear being rejected by others. They will also reject themselves. It is this self-rejection that prepares their hearts to receive the next principality's lies into their thoughts.

Principality (Rule)

The human spirit is ready and willing to serve God. People cannot fall into degradation and sin as long as their conscience (the mind of the spirit) is awake to righteousness (see 1 Cor. 15:34; 1 John 3:9).

Delilah lulled Samson to sleep on her knees as she enticed him with her wiles (see Judg. 16:19). Likewise, the spirit of *slumber* must subdue people's spirits and put them to sleep to the reality of what they are being seduced into before they will yield to satan's temptations (see Rom. 11:8). As people's consciences becomes quieted, the spirit of whoredoms entices them with the imaginations of the pleasures of sin (see Hos. 5:4).

Power (Authority)

After people have yielded to the spirit of *whoredoms*, regardless if by mental consent or through sexual contact, they become whoredom's servant (see Matt. 5:27-28). *"...Whosoever commits sin is the servant of sin"* (John 8:34). Likewise, Paul said, *"To whom ye yield yourselves to obey, his servants ye are to whom ye obey..."* (Rom. 6:16).

This spirit manifests itself in many different ways: adultery, fornication, homosexuality, masturbation, pornography, lasciviousness, and evil concupiscence. Also, when demons from other sin categories are involved in such immoral behavior, then other acts such as exposing oneself publicly, rape, and sadism may occur (more about spirits from different categories working together later).

Might

When the spirit of whoredoms stimulates people to yield to the entice-ment of sensual pleasures, the powerful spirit of *gluttony* begins working. *This demon is the enemy of all moderation.* He works to addict people through their passions. Combining obsessive and compulsive behavior, this foul spirit enslaves people through their passions and lusts.

A spirit of gluttony is not limited to compelling people to overeat. Gluti-nous people are those given to sensuous appetites. Whether they habitu-ally indulge in excessive food, drink, sex, or any other passionate lust, this is the work of a spirit of gluttony (see Prov. 30:20; Luke 21:34).

Dominion (Mastery)

As people impulsively and compulsively indulge their fleshly appetites, the spirit of *guilt* condemns them. This demon obtains mastery over their minds to sever and keep them separated from God (see Gen. 3:8; Isa. 59:1-2).

True conviction (from the human spirit or from the Spirit of Truth) is healthy and good. Through faith in the cleansing blood of Jesus, confession of sin frees people from conviction. The purpose of true conviction is to bring people to repentance and, through faith, restore them to God (see Acts 2:37-38, 15:9; Heb. 9:14).

In contrast to this, the spirit of guilt makes people feel guilty, con-demned, and unworthy. Also, *confession will not make a demon of guilt leave.* Instead, he must be cast out. The objective of a spirit of guilt is to make people feel ashamed, unworthy, and inferior. He tries to make them feel hopelessly bad and to drive them away from God and His mercy.

Before salvation, the Holy Spirit convicts people of being sinners, try-ing to persuade them to repent. After they are redeemed, the Holy Spirit identifies specific wrongs, sins, faults, and failings and points them out so they will repent of them. God convicts people of their transgressions to bring them to repentance (see 2 Cor. 7:9-11).

On the other hand, the unclean spirit of guilt strives to make people regard themselves as bad, or no good. This demon suggests to his victims that since they are hopeless, they may as well persist in sinning (see Jer. 18:12). Guilt continually accuses people of *being* evil; God and the human spirit convict people when they *do* evil.

Guilt unfairly condemns, making people feel dirty or unworthy and ashamed, even after they are, in truth, clean. Guilt will often make people feel guilty even about such activities as buying shoes, eating food, or doing other essential things. An evil spirit of guilt may keep people from resting when they should, telling them they should be doing something useful. A spirit of guilt opposes faith, opening people's hearts to the fear of punishment.

When people are living in sin, indulging their fleshly appetites in different kinds of sexual sin, satan inflames their imaginations and emotions to drive them ever deeper into bondage. But, often, when they repent and turn to God, the *"enemy of all righteousness"* will reverse his tactics and suppress their normal sexual desires. The same couple that enjoyed fornicating together outside of marriage, once they are married, will usually have trouble in their sexual relationship. By preventing one or both of them from rendering *"due benevolence,"* satan attempts to destroy their God-given right to enjoy one another, and he attempts to weaken or break their emotional bond of love (see Acts 13:10; Rom. 7:19-21; 1 Cor. 7:2-5).

In summary, we observed that a spirit of *rejection* influences people to yield to a spirit of *slumber*. This causes the Wheel of Nature to begin turning, bringing people into fornication. The spirit of *whoredoms*, followed by *gluttony*, defiles people's conscience and opens their minds to the dominion of the spirit of *guilt*. Feeling guilty, they are condemned in their hearts and further separated from God—who alone can heal the wounds that rejection and guilt inflict upon people's souls (see Heb. 9:14).

When men and women attempt to change and live righteously, satan, who is the enemy of all righteousness, fights against them by diverting, perverting, or suppressing their normal sexual desires and tries to use guilt and offense to hinder their marriage.

In the next chapter, we will look more closely at the spirit of guilt and his insidious works. As we examine the scorpion further, we will see how this spirit causes the Wheel of Nature to continue its rotation.

God has provided a cure for humanity's sinful condition in the cross of His Son, Jesus. Since people's immoral dilemma stems from a low self-image received by rejection, it is obvious that the immediate remedy people need is acceptance.

This is precisely what God does through the cross of Christ. When people come to God through Christ, before anything else, *God assures them that they are accepted by Him. They are accepted in the Beloved by adoption into the family of God* (see Eph. 1:5-6). Through God's acceptance people are transformed into His likeness. There is no better self-image that people can have than to see themselves as those chosen, accepted, and beloved of God (see Gen. 1:27; Rom. 8:29; 2 Cor. 3:18).

Parental (and other) rejection is healed as people forgive their parents and all others who have offended them. God has promised to provide the love and acceptance their parents were unable, or unwilling, to supply: *"When my father and my mother forsake me, then the Lord will take me up"* (Ps. 27:10; see also Ps. 147:3).

Through confession of sin and faith in the blood of Jesus, people's consciences are cleansed from dead works that they may serve the living God. Because they are made free from the guilt that condemned them, they can have confidence toward God (see Heb. 9:14; 1 John 1:9, 3:21).

When people learn to look to God to satisfy all their needs and desires, they will find an antidote for every one of satan's poisonous devices. As they learn to appropriate all that God has provided through the cross, truly, they shall be healed.

Sin—Whoremonger

Lust (Eye)—Desire to Conquer
Root (Leg)—Low Self-Image
Branch (Motion)—Inordinate (Passionate) Affection

Spirits

Principality (Rule)—Slumber
Power (Authority)—Whoredoms
Might (Miracle Power)—Gluttony
Dominion (Mastery)—Guilt

Fruits

Compulsive and impulsive sexual behavior; Vile, excessive affections

Some Common Sins in this Category:

Adultery; Fornication; Uncleanliness; Lasciviousness;
Homosexual acts; Fetishism; Overeating

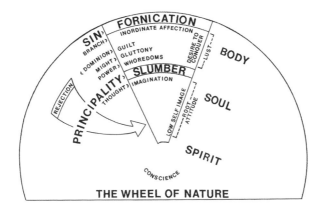

THE WHEEL OF NATURE

Chapter 13

THE FEARFUL AND AFRAID

*But the **fearful**, and unbelieving, and abominable, and murderers, and whoremongers, and sorcerers, and idolaters, and all liars, shall have their part in the lake which burneth with fire and brimstone...* (Revelation 21:8).

As we examine the sin of fearfulness, the question naturally arises: *"Why is yielding to fear considered sinful conduct?"* The answer is simple: *"Whatsoever is not of faith is sin"* (Rom. 14:23). Being fearful (having an attitude of dread) is not only sin, it is the exact opposite of faith.

Both fear and faith have an expectancy of something happening in the future. Faith produces an anticipation of something good happening—fear produces an apprehension of something bad. Faith hopes for the best. Fear expects the worst. Thus being apprehensive and worrying about the future, dreading the worst to come, is the opposite of faith and is sin (see Matt. 8:26; Rom. 8:24-25).

Everyone experiences fear at one time or another, and it is perfectly natural to be afraid of being hurt or of dying. But the Bible says that Jesus died so *"that through death he might...deliver them who through fear of death were all their lifetime subject to bondage"* (Heb. 2:14-15). So, obviously, God does not want us to be afraid of death.

Nevertheless, when people's consciences are defiled by sin, a *spirit of guilt* will make them feel condemned. This opens their hearts to the fear of punishment, or *fear of death* (see 1 John 3:20). The human spirit, which is created in God's likeness, instinctively knows that the *"wages of sin is death..."* (Rom. 6:23).

When people feel guilty (whether the guilt is real or imagined) they expect punishment. The fear of punishment, or more accurately, the fear of death, is the *"leg"* of the scorpion within humanity. This root attitude motivates people to protect themselves and preserve their lives. The drive to save self is one of humanity's strongest basic instincts.

All flesh loves life, and indeed, life is a priceless possession. If this passion is fulfilled through Christ, it is good (see Gal. 2:20; 1 Pet. 3:10). True, abundant life is only obtained through a close relationship with God through Christ. John said, *"This is life eternal, that they may know Thee, the only true God, and Jesus Christ, whom Thou hast sent"* (John 17:3).

Likewise, Jesus said that He would give His followers, *"life... more abundantly,"* but to obtain it they must submit their wills to Him and lay down their lives in relation to this world (see Luke 14:33; John 10:10). Eternal life is only available through the cross:

> *And he that taketh not his cross, and followeth after Me, is not worthy of Me. He that findeth his life shall lose it: and he that loseth his life for My sake shall find it* (Matthew 10:38-39).

Proverbs 9:10, which says, *"The fear of the Lord is the beginning of wisdom...,"* and Psalm 19:9, which says, *"The fear of the Lord is clean...,"* show that all fear is not sin. But, as we have seen, most of the dread people have in their hearts *is* sin, and some of it is even a direct result of sin! This is because when people sin they transgress God's Law of Love. Unloving action always floods the conscience with guilt, and guilty people fear they will be exposed and punished. When Adam sinned and heard God coming, he immediately hid himself out of fear (see Gen. 3:10).

We see this foreboding in nations as they prepare defensively for war, the collective conscience of the nations' populace perceiving and agreeing that punishment is eminent. *"The wicked flee when no man pursueth: but the righteous are bold as a lion"* (Prov. 28:1).

Families of criminals and alcoholics live in constant dread. They are afraid the family unit will be broken apart because of the iniquity that is in their midst. Besides violence and abuse from within, arrest, divorce, or even death threatens the security of both children and adults.

We have already discussed the emotional bond of affection formed between two people as a result of positional relationship. As a husband rules his family in love, his wife responds in her affections, forming a bond of love. Paul called this love, *"The bond of perfectness"* (Col. 3:14).

In like manner, in a family ruled by the principality of fear (dread), an emotional bond is formed through fear! This is the bond (bondage) that holds marriages and other relationships together when a dominating person abuses his or her partner. Regardless of whether this mistreatment is with verbal abuse or physical blows, the demons work to instill bondage in those subjected to abuse.

This is the reason God gives His permission for a troubled person to leave an abusive spouse under such conditions (see 1 Cor. 7:15). The Word of God specifically releases Christians from the authority of a spirit of bondage when abuse is present. *"...A brother or a sister is not under bondage in such cases: but God hath called us to peace"* (1 Cor. 7:15).

Four Defense Mechanisms

Life means different things to different people. Jesus said, *"Take heed, and beware of covetousness: for a man's life consisteth not in the abundance of the things which he possesseth"* (Luke 12:15), but if people believe that it does, they will fear losing their worldly goods. They will dread the thought of having to do without the things they are accustomed to. Therefore, they will take great pains to shield themselves from losing them.

In the natural world, people engineer many ways to protect themselves from loss. Insurance, safes, iron bars, keyed locks, high walls, and barbed fences are all common means of protection. Military forces, policemen, and fire departments all serve to prevent or stop calamity from robbing people of their goods, or even their lives.

People also develop an array of defensive mechanisms to keep themselves from experiencing pain and grief in the realm of the soul. Just as people react quickly to the threat of fire and theft, they defend their words and deeds as well. They also react defensively when their motives or actions are questioned or their reputation is threatened.

People develop *conditioned responses* to these threats, whether they are real or imagined. The defense mechanisms they develop to protect themselves and safeguard both their images and the natural aspects of their lives have much to do with shaping their personalities.

There are four primary defense mechanisms developed by people as they mature (there are others, like overeating, alcoholism, or even workaholism, but these are often just adaptations of the basic four). Although those who use these mechanisms erect them for defense, they actually become prison walls, restricting and hindering their interaction with others. They prevent those who are outside from intruding, it is true, but they also take away the liberty of those who are inside and, thus, rob them of many of life's real pleasures.

The *first* of these walls is to *withdraw* or *retreat* in an attempt to avoid whatever appears threatening. Cowardliness is one manifestation of this form of protective shield (see Prov. 22:13). A biblical example of this can be seen in the story of Gideon (see Judg. 6:11-15). Gideon had the potential to be a mighty man of valor, but he was hiding from his enemies. In his faithlessness, he said God had forsaken Israel. His excuse for not obeying the angel that visited him was that his family was poor and that he was the least of them. But when he ceased acting fearfully and faced what he feared, God gave him complete victory over his enemies.

Daydreaming is another way of retreating. The imaginary world of fantasy, so natural to a child, becomes a means of escape for adults who fear to face reality. Daydreams, romance novels, and soap operas provide a place to live that seems far more pleasant than the real world filled with barbed threats and abusive situations, but the illusion is deceptive and short-lived.

The defense mechanisms of fear have many disguises. Some people camouflage themselves with shyness, quietly attempting to go unnoticed as the world passes them by, but inwardly, they are crying out for love and recognition.

False or nervous laughter is another way of covering the sense of inadequacy or inferiority. If people present themselves to others with lightness, there is less threat that they will feel rejected if they are not taken seriously.

The *second* of these prison walls is to *stubbornly resist* anything that threatens people's way of life. Through obstinate self-will, these people stubbornly defend their right to have their own way. By refusing to submit their will to others, they ignore any power or authority that would change it or them. This includes learning to *"tune people out"* of their consciousness to avoid being controlled by them (see Prov. 7:10-11).

The *third* defense is to *outwit* or *outmaneuver* the threatening situation or person by attempting to use superior wisdom. Using charm, wit, shrewdness, cunning, or even deception, some people just try to outsmart their opponents (see 1 Sam. 21:12-15; Prov. 26:16).

The *fourth* defense mechanism is to *attack* by force and power. Such people will use threats, criticisms, accusations, or anything else that will invoke fear or guilt in others. Anything that will intimidate their adversaries, to cause their enemies' retreat instead of their own, is subject to being used to ensure survival (see Ezra 4:23). Each of these last three defense mechanisms will be briefly discussed in the next three chapters respectively.

Although people normally develop all four of these conditioned responses as they mature, they usually cultivate one to a much greater degree than the others. They depend upon it as their first line of defense.

They only revert to one of the others when their first shield appears insufficient to save them.

It is not uncommon for people to develop various combinations of these protective devices as well. They often combine the first two. They first withdraw from whatever appears to threaten them; then they simply deny that anything is wrong. In their desperate attempts to avoid confrontation, they refuse to acknowledge that anything is out of order. They subconsciously deny the truth both to themselves and others.

Likewise, the second two are often combined. Using cunning and wisdom, often unconsciously, they scorn and criticize (attack) their opponents. These people try to put their enemies, or whoever is perceived as a threat to their way of life, on the defensive.

Principality (Rule)

The inherent love of life is the "eye" of the scorpion that satan uses. His purpose is to draw people into the web of deception he weaves as he invokes apprehension in their hearts. The spirit of *fear (dread)* works to influence their thoughts to bring them into subjection to the spirit of bondage.

Power (Authority)

When people give place to satan by avoiding confrontation or by compromising through fear, they yield their members to a spirit of *bondage* (see Eph. 4:27). Through the Law of Dominion, this spirit is then authorized to continue humbling those he has bound. This spirit compels his victims to yield each time they encounter a circumstance in which they feel apprehensive or threatened.

Might

Once the spirit of bondage gains authority to bind people, the powerful spirit of *anxiety* begins his work. This demon enslaves people through the power of their own passions.

There are over 200 different manifestations of the spirit of anxiety that have been classified by psychiatrists. These strong fears are called phobias. A phobia is a strong, binding, inhibiting, terrifying emotion that controls people in certain circumstances. These feelings of panic or horror may be stimulated by objects, sounds, people, smells, colors, or even by thoughts and imaginations. The list of things that the spirit of anxiety can use to open his victims' hearts is endless. A description of the workings of this spirit is found in Psalm 55:3-6:

> *Because of the voice of the enemy, because of the oppression of the wicked: for they cast iniquity upon me, and in wrath they hate me. My heart is sore pained within me: and the terrors of death are fallen upon me. Fearfulness and trembling are come upon me, and horror hath overwhelmed me. And I said, Oh that I had wings like a dove! for then would I fly away, and be at rest* (Psalm 55:3-6).

The *voices* of the oppressing spirits, the *paranoia* (*"they hate me"*), the *quickening of the heart rate* and the *fear of death*, are all normal symptoms of an anxiety (panic) attack. The psalmist's *"trembling"* at some imagined horror, his being *"overwhelmed"* by the passion of great fear, and his *wishing in vain to be able to fly away and escape* are all direct results of an evil spirit of anxiety (terror) dwelling within.

Dominion (Mastery)

Once the powerful spirit of anxiety has gained a stronghold in people's minds, his victims are subject to the spirit of *confusion*. This is the spirit that works insanity in many of his captives (see Ps. 44:14-16; James 3:16).

It is enlightening to examine the various passages of Scripture where Jesus cast the demons out of the insane man in the land of the Gadarenes (see Luke 8:26-39). Luke recorded that the man had demons, went naked, lived in a graveyard, and possessed superhuman strength, and Mark told us that no man could bind or tame him (see Mark 5:2-5). The Gadarenes were incapable of overcoming the stubborn self-will of this lunatic.

When Jesus asked the demons their name, their answer was unique. They said their name was Legion because there were so many of them. This information is significant because it reveals that as people repeatedly yield their members to sin, the quantity of demons increase. *The demons' ability to exercise control in people's lives is directly proportional to their numbers* (see Deut. 32:30-36; Luke 11:26).

These unclean spirits had effectively suppressed and displaced this man's spirit and were in complete control of his entire consciousness. By dwelling in his flesh and controlling him through his carnal mind, they tormented him both physically and mentally.

When Jesus commanded them to leave, they entered a herd of swine nearby and caused about 2,000 of them to drown. The hogs reacted to the demons' compulsive influence and stampeded (see Mark 5:13).

The primary emotion that causes animals to stampede is fear. The swine's irrational act of drowning themselves was a direct result of the spirits of anxiety (terror) and confusion working together to destroy whatever vessels they were in (see 1 John 4:18).

This is confirmed further as we observe what these same spirits did later. When the townspeople came out to see for themselves the scene described by the swine herders, the evil spirits swarmed them. When these people saw Jesus counseling the now sane, former lunatic, they were *"taken with great fear."* The same demons which drowned the swine entered the sightseers and caused them to be terrified of Jesus (see Luke 8:37).

People have a natural fear of the unknown, and 2,000 hogs are worth a lot of money. The demons used the people's intrinsic fear of the supernatural, along with the implied threat of losing more income, to rob them. They worked, through the fear of death (loss) to open the peoples' hearts to the unclean spirits of bondage. In this way, the demons kept the Gadarenes bound to the beggarly elements of this world.

The Gadarenes' natural fear of the unknown, and their trust in material resources instead of the power of God so vividly demonstrated by Jesus, opened their carnal minds to fear. This dread and the resultant bondage which accompanied it allowed the powerful spirits of anxiety to invade the townspeople. The unclean spirits bound the astonished people's proper response toward God and compelled them to react with panic.

Notice the counsel Jesus gave the newly liberated man. He was not allowed to follow Him. Instead, Jesus sent him back to his own house. *To help him overcome his phobias, Jesus made him go and face the people, places, and things he had been unable to confront or endure before.* He obeyed; therefore, his actions completed the healing process that Jesus started.

> *Commit thy works unto the Lord, and thy thoughts shall be established* (Proverbs 16:3).

The opposite of fear is faith. Without believing the Lord's counsel and obeying His word, this man would have been easy prey for satan. These same spirits would have returned and reclaimed the house (person) they had lived in for so long (see Luke 11:24-26).

Covenant Principles

The fear of the Lord is the beginning of wisdom. The love of God is the end of wisdom. To love God is to obey Him (see Prov. 9:10; 1 John 5:3). To obey God is to become servant to Him by the same Law of Dominion that subjects people to demon forces. Being subject to God entitles people to His protection through *the principles of covenant.*

> *By humility and the fear of the Lord are riches, and honour, and life* (Proverbs 22:4).

When Israel first invaded Canaan, a company of Gibeonites met Joshua. These men used deception and convinced him to make a treaty with them. After he agreed with them, he was bound by his covenant. Even though they were his enemies, he still had to keep his word. Later, when the Philistines attacked these former enemies of Israel, as a result of his agreement, Joshua defended them. Because the men of Gibeon submitted themselves to his rule, he was obligated to fight for them when they were in trouble. Similarly, our Joshua (Jesus) defends us when we are under attack because of His covenant with us (see Josh. 9:11-27, 10:3-8; Ps. 94:22-23).

Second Chronicles 18:3 reveals this important aspect of a covenant relationship. Jehoshaphat told Ahab: *"I am as thou art, and my people as thy people; and we will be with thee in the war."*

When a person is in authority, he is responsible for all who are in covenant agreement and submitted to him. *The Universal Law of Stewardship is: "Unto whomsoever much is given, of him shall be much required"* (Luke 12:48). This Law requires all who are in authority to be good, faithful stewards of that which has been committed to their trust. God is unfailingly faithful, so He is the perfect example of a good steward. Therefore, delivered people are safe under His protection.[1]

God, through His covenant with humanity, has given His Spirit, *"to them that obey Him"* (Acts 5:32). Paul said in Romans 8:15, *"Ye have not received the spirit of bondage again to fear; but ye have received the Spirit of adoption..."* The Spirit of Adoption is not, *"the spirit of fear; but the spirit of power, and of love, and of a sound mind"* (2 Tim. 1:7). God's antidote for the serpent's poison and the scorpion's sting is revealed in these Scriptures.

The *principality* of fear (dread) is overruled by the *Spirit of Adoption.* As obedient children of God, people should have no fear of death, for to die is gain (see Phil. 1:21).

The *power* (authority) of the spirit of bondage is annulled, for *"...Where the Spirit of the Lord is, there is liberty"* (2 Cor. 3:17). Instead of bondage, Christians have access to the *Spirit of Power.* God has given His children power and authority over all their enemies' power (see Luke 10:19).

The *might* of the spirit of anxiety becomes annihilated for *"There is no fear* [terror] *in love; but* [the Spirit of] *perfect love casteth out fear; because fear hath torment..."* (1 John 4:18). To love God is to obey Him, and to be obedient is to be filled with confidence (see 1 John 5:3, 3:21-22).

Finally, instead of being under the *dominion* and mastery of the spirit of confusion, God's children have the *Spirit of a sound mind*, even the mind of Christ (see 1 Cor. 2:16). Through the cross of Christ, all things are ours! God has covenanted to make all things work together for our good (see Rom. 8:28; 1 Cor. 3:21-23).

Hallelujah! Our victorious Captain has led captivity captive and given us victory over our emotions. Fear has no rightful place in us. Refuse to be *"terrified by your adversaries"* (Phil. 1:28), for *"If God be for us, who can be against us?"* (Rom. 8:31)

In summary, we can see that the *spirit of fear (dread)* works in people's thoughts to influence them to yield to the *spirit of bondage*. Once they are bound, the *powerful spirit of anxiety, or terror*, works through their emotions to bring them under the *dominion*, or *mastery*, of the *spirit of confusion*. No longer in full control of their own mind, they are then subject to the influence of the next principality, as the Wheel of Nature continues to roll. We will see how the spirit of confusion works to make people's minds receptive to the next principality in the following chapter.

Endnote

1. For more on this, see the Law of Stewardship in the endnotes of Chapter 3 (pages 32-33).

Sin—Fearful

Lust (Eye)—Love of Life

Root (Leg)—Fear of Death

Branch (Motion)—Faithlessness (Cowardliness)

Spirits

Principality (Rule)—Fear (Dread)

Power (Authority)—Bondage

Might (Miracle Power)—Anxiety (Terror)

Dominion (Mastery)—Confusion

Fruits

Dismay; Cowardice; Inhibitions; Insanity; Torment

Some Common Sins in this Category

Giving place (Fear of man, etc.); Superstitions; Instability

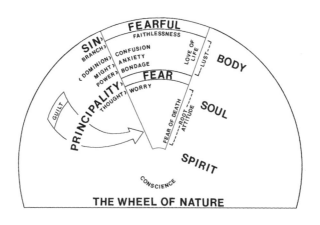

THE WHEEL OF NATURE

Chapter 14

HARDEN NOT YOUR HEART

*But the fearful, and **unbelieving**, and abominable, and murderers, and whoremongers, and sorcerers, and idolaters, and all liars, shall have their part in the lake which burneth with fire and brimstone...* (Revelation 21:8).

A s we continue our investigation, please note that the further the Wheel travels, the more spirits there are that influence its rotation. So far, at this point, we have three dominion spirits—rejection, guilt, and confusion—along with various principalities, powers, and mights, all working together to cause its perpetual motion. When these demons obtain a grip upon people's minds, they contribute the necessary force to make the Wheel continue its somewhat slow, but relentless progress.

Each of these dominion spirits work through the subconscious, carnal mind to develop certain patterns of thought in the conscious mind. Their purpose is to produce habitual and repetitive sin. By creating and maintaining conditioned responses, they cause their victims to commit the same sins over and over.

The spirits of confusion, working in conjunction with rejection, guilt, fear, and several other spirits, are no exception. These spirits repeatedly inject worrisome, conflicting, and confusing thoughts into people's conscious minds to bring them deeper and further into bondage.

These unclean spirits work their nature within people to bring them into captivity and, in the process, cause them to conform to satan's despicable image. The spirit of confusion wars against his victims' sound mind to drive them to sin and, when possible, into insanity. Satan is the epitome of insanity. Who but an insane fool would rebel against the Almighty God, stubbornly struggling to exalt his own will above God's? (See Isaiah 14:12-15.)

To answer this question, we will examine the effects that the spirit of confusion had on the insane man of the Gadarenes, who we discussed in the last chapter (see Luke 8:27-29). One of the results of harboring fear in the thoughts, with the resulting confusion it breeds, is the development of the defense mechanism of stubbornness. The Gadarene lunatic, who was tormented by fear, is a perfect example.

The Gadarenes were unable to overcome his obstinate self-will. He chose nakedness over clothing and tombs for a home. He even broke chains off his hands and feet as he stubbornly resisted all external control over his life.

Evil, stubborn self-will is symptomatic of demonic control. When a spirit of confusion has displaced people's human spirit, their rational minds cannot influence their behavior as it should. Even the God-given, sound mind of Christ cannot control their lives. Once people have yielded themselves to satan, *he* is in control.

The carnal mind is the enemy of God because of its reverse design. It is through this mind that demon forces work their evil devices. By convincing people to surrender to the desires of their flesh and carnal minds, satan can close their ears to God's Word. If people cannot hear God, they cannot do His will (see John 8:43-44). Jesus said:

> *As I hear, I judge: and My judgment is just; because I seek not Mine own will, but the will of the Father which hath sent Me* (John 5:30).

When people are able to hear with their whole hearts, they can and will submit to His Word. This allows God to work His righteousness in them. When people desire God's will for themselves, they have the proper attitude toward life, and they will hear and judge rightly.

"So then faith cometh by hearing, and hearing by the word of God" (Rom. 10:17). Conversely, unbelief comes by *not* hearing. To keep from hearing, people must stubbornly close their ears. God's Word is being broadcast continually:

> *The heavens declare the glory of God; and the firmament sheweth His handiwork. Day unto day uttereth speech, and night unto night sheweth knowledge. There is no speech nor language, where their voice is not heard* (Psalm 19:1-3).

> *But I say, Have they not heard* [His Word]*? Yes verily, their sound went into all the earth, and their words unto the ends of the world* (Romans 10:18).

To close the ears to God is unbelief. Unbelief is not doubt nor the inability to believe. *Unbelief is stubborn refusal to hear!* Stubborn refusal to hear is the result of being self-willed. Self-will is the motivating "leg" of the scorpion in humanity.

People's lives are supposed to be centered on God. But when their attitudes are selfish, they want to take God's place. *They* want to be the center. They even want God to serve them! This evil root motivates people to pursue their own pleasure instead of their Creator's (see 2 Tim. 3:4; Rev. 4:11). It causes them to exalt their own selfish will above His perfect will.

When people are obsessed with carnal lusts, they will honor their own will above His. Likewise, they will strive to obtain the honor of other people. Wanting others to exalt them and esteem them worthy of honor makes them try to please others instead of God. In this way, people become people-pleasers instead of God-pleasers (see Gal. 1:10).

The "eye" of the scorpion is the desire for the honor of man. Jesus said, *"How can ye believe, which receive honor one of another, and seek not the honor that cometh from God only?"* (John 5:44)

A better understanding of how the desire for honor and the sin of unbelief correlate with each other can be obtained by examining Samuel's rebuke of Saul in Scripture. In the confrontation between these two men, Samuel accused Saul of not obeying God's commandment. Saul stubbornly contended that he *had* obeyed, even though the facts denied his allegations.

Saul's excuse for his disobedience was that, although he had not fully obeyed, he fully intended to do so, later. He reasoned that he could please God by offering Him the sheep he had spared as a sacrifice. Samuel's response to Saul's stubborn disobedience and denial reveals the hidden motive behind Saul's sin:

> *And Samuel said, "Hath the Lord as great delight in burnt offerings and sacrifices, as in obeying the voice of the Lord? Behold, to obey is better than sacrifice, and to hearken than the fat of rams. For rebellion is as the sin of witchcraft, and stubbornness is as iniquity and idolatry. Because thou hast rejected the word of the Lord, He hath also rejected thee from being king." And Saul said unto Samuel, "I have sinned: for I have transgressed the commandment of the Lord, and thy words: because I feared the people, and obeyed their voice..." Then he said, "I have sinned: yet honour me now, I pray thee, before the elders of my people, and before Israel..."* (1 Samuel 15:22-30).

When Saul faced the threat of losing the honor of his men, he disobeyed God. *You cannot serve God and people any more than you can serve God and mammon.* Samuel called Saul's actions iniquity (unbelief) and idolatry.

Proverbs 29:25 warns, *"The fear of man bringeth a snare...."* It does not matter if people's apprehension is the fear of rejection, the fear of the loss of the honor of others, or the fear of others' anger—all three bring them into the *"bond of iniquity,"* or unbelief.

For example, Simon the sorcerer resorted to bribery in an attempt to keep Samaria's honor. The people there held him in high regard for a long time because of his sorceries. But when Peter came to Samaria immediately after Philip's revival, he laid his hands on the people and they received the Holy Spirit and spoke in tongues. When Simon the sorcerer saw this demonstration of God's power, he was envious and wanted it for himself. His desire for spiritual power was selfish. His purpose was not to bless the people, but to retain their honor. Peter read his heart and perceived that his motive was evil, so he rebuked him (see Acts 8:5-23).

This is not an isolated case. The desire for God's power is evident in many Christians today. Why? Does it stem from a deep love for God's sheep, from a desire to supply their many needs, or is it just a carnal lust for power? Desiring spiritual power to control people and obtain their honor is evil.

We previously learned that one aspect of idolatry is the desire for the envy, or worship, of peers. This desire to be highly esteemed and honored among their peers entices people to come down from the cross and become competitors with God. But they cannot contend for the praise of people and still please God. God's children cannot compete with Him and serve Him at the same time.

One of the carnal mind's natures is to crave worship, but yielding to its demands is suicide (see Acts 8:20; Rom. 8:5-6). People must look to God alone for honor. *Jesus said, "...If any man serve Me, him will my Father honor"* (John 12:26). This statement, along with John 5:44, shows that it is not wrong to desire God's honor, but it *is* wrong to desire honor from others.

Likewise, Jesus did not say it is wrong to *have* the honor of people; He said it is evil to *seek* the honor of people. For instance, Jesus said, *"A prophet is not without honour, save in his own country, and in his own house"* (Matt. 13:57). Paul said:

[God will] *render to every man according to his deeds: To them who by patient continuance in well doing seek* [God] *for glory and honour and immortality,* [they will obtain] *eternal life* (Romans 2:6-7).

As always, we can see that it is not people's desires, but rather by what and how they are fulfilled that determines whether their deeds are sinful or righteous. To try to obtain honor on a horizontal level, that is, from others, is sin.

Christians obtain God's honor by serving Him. They can only serve God from one place—the cross. They must be deaf to the world's demands upon them if they really want to please God. When they are deaf to the demands of their flesh and carnal mind, they can hear God (see Gal. 1:10). Only when they are truly and solely desiring His will for themselves will their hearts be open to hear. This singleness of desire is what Jesus referred to in Matthew 6:22, *"The light of the body is the eye: if therefore thine eye* [desire] *be single, thy whole body shall be full of light."*

Principality (Rule)

Since the human spirit desires to please and serve God, satan must pervert people's minds with a distorted attitude before he can control their lives. By influencing them to value the honor of their peers, he can gain control over them by prompting them to sin through unbelief. The principality satan sends to do this work is a ***perverse*** spirit (see Isa. 19:14).

Paul, in Acts 20:30, warned the Ephesian church's elders that men would arise and speak perverse things to draw away disciples after themselves. This proselytizing is common in the Church today. Paul also warned the Church about perverse disputing among people in First Timothy 6:3-5. We can see both of these aspects of a perverse spirit in Luke 9:49-50:

And John answered and said, "Master, we saw one casting out devils in Thy name; and we forbad him, because he followeth

*not with us." And Jesus said unto him, "Forbid him not; for he
that is not against us is for us"* (Luke 9:49-50).

This desire for followers is seen in some Christians as they gather
admirers around themselves within the local assembly. Others persuade
their deceived supporters to leave with them to start a new work. Often
this is done in the guise of following after *"the deep things of God"* (1 Cor.
2:10).

Although God must at times deliver His people from religious or
institutional bondage, they should be vigilant to guard against following a
person instead of God. Paul told his converts to follow him as he followed
Christ (see 1 Cor. 11:1). He specifically said that he did not seek glory or
honor from his followers:

> *Nor of men sought we glory, neither of you, nor yet of others,
> when we might have been burdensome, as the apostles of Christ*
> (1 Thessalonians 2:6).

Jesus did not try to persuade people to come after Him. He simply led
those who were wise enough to follow. He did not speak to please itch-
ing ears, nor was He offended when people took offense at His Word (see
Matt. 15:12-14; 2 Tim. 4:3).

Likewise, when Paul was rejected as an apostle by the Corinthians, he
was not overly disturbed. Paul refused to place undue importance on their
opinion of him. His heart was free from the desire for people's honor (see
1 Cor. 4:3).

Jesus rebuked His disciples for listening to a perverse spirit when they
could not deliver a deaf boy from demon possession in Luke 9:41: *"And
Jesus said, 'O faithless and perverse generation, how long shall I be with you,
and suffer you?'"*

When they asked Jesus why they could not deliver the boy, He
answered, *"Because of your unbelief..."* (Matt. 17:20). Their faithlessness was
the result of a perverse desire for the honor of their peers. This can be seen

by examining several Scriptures immediately following Christ's rebuke of the disciples:

> *"Let these sayings sink down into your ears: for the Son of man shall be delivered unto the hands of men." But they understood not this saying, and it was hid from them, that they perceived it not: and they feared to ask Him of that saying* (Luke 9:44-45).

Power (Authority)

In this saying, Jesus revealed his own position in regard to the world. In His heart He was already on the cross, not regarding or seeking people's honor. But His disciples could not perceive or understand why He said that He would be delivered into the hands of men. They could not hear Him because they were still under the influence of a perverse spirit. A *deaf and dumb* spirit had closed their ears. They could not perceive (hear with their hearts) or receive this saying because it was contrary to their own desires. Their self-will would not allow them to receive the truth (see Matt. 16:23; Luke 9:45).

Jesus dealt further with their wrong values by confronting them concerning their ambition to be the greatest. He presented a child to them in a "show and tell" lesson and said, *"He that is least among you all* [as a child is], *the same shall be great"* (Luke 9:48).

Might

Once a deaf and dumb spirit succeeds in closing people's ears to God, a powerful spirit of *slothfulness* will enter them. This demon's purpose is to prevent people from working out God's perfect will for themselves (see Prov. 26:16, 12:24; Rom. 12:1-2; Phil. 2:12).

Some who have this spirit are actually hard workers in the natural, but they are lazy in spiritual things. They are apathetic when it comes to doing the things that please God, such as worship and prayer. This spirit resists activity that would be profitable to people's families, churches, communities, or countries. He greatly influences people to fulfill the selfish desires of their flesh and carnal mind at the expense of their own spirit's welfare (see Prov. 18:9, 21:25-26, 26:16).

Dominion (Mastery)

The final *mastery* in this area of life is obtained by a spirit of **defiance**. This dominion adamantly resists the conviction of its victims' consciences. It defies all righteousness, turning its hosts into selfish, self-willed, self-centered people. It compels them to place their own personal desires and opinions ahead of all authority ordained of God.

This alliance of perversion, deafness, slothfulness, and defiance can be seen in Zechariah 7:11-12:

> *But they refused to hearken* [perversion], *and pulled away the shoulder, and stopped their ears* [deafness], *that they should not hear* [slothfulness]. *Yea, they made their hearts as an adamant stone* [defiance], *lest they should hear the law, and the words which the Lord of hosts hath sent in His spirit by the former prophets: therefore came a great wrath from the Lord of Hosts* (Zechariah 7:11-12).

Here, as in Hebrews 3:11-12, we encounter the inevitable results of unbelief—namely, to suffer God's wrath. *When people are rejected by God, they lose all hope of obtaining His promises.* The promises they had before they exercised their obstinate refusal to hear and obey God's Word are annulled.

A careful study of the deliverance of the young lad mentioned earlier, whom Jesus healed of deafness, will reveal God's cure for the sin of unbelief. Mark 9:21-25 records that Jesus asked the boy's father a rather revealing question:

> [Jesus asked,] *"How long is it ago since this* [deafness] *came unto him?" And* [the father] *said, "Of a child* [Greek: infant]*…but if Thou canst do anything, have compassion on us, and help us." Jesus said unto him, "If thou canst believe, all things are possible to him that believeth." And straightway the father of the child cried out, and said with tears, "Lord, I believe; help Thou mine unbelief." When Jesus saw that the people came running together, He rebuked the foul spirit, saying unto him, "Thou dumb and deaf spirit, I charge thee, come out of him, and enter no more into him"* (Mark 9:21-25).

It is very important to see Jesus' method of dealing with this spirit. *Notice that He did not rebuke the demon until He had disarmed him.* Jesus did this by taking away the unclean spirit's right to close the boy's ears.

Jesus revealed the demon's source (the father's sin), and exposed the root of the boy's problem in the process. By counseling the boy's father and drawing out a confession of unbelief from him (*"the father…said with tears…help Thou mine unbelief"*), He annulled the covenant of sin the boy was born under (see Lev. 26:39-42).

This repentance and confession released the son from the generational curse received through his father's sin. *The father had refused to hear; as a result, the son could not hear!* Unless the sins of the fathers are repented of, they are visited upon the children and upon their future generations (see Exod. 34:7).

Jesus mastered the desire for honor in His own life by first defeating the perverse spirit in his own mind. As a result, through the Law of Dominion, Jesus had dominion over this demon and all other spirits under this demon's authority (see 2 Cor. 10:5-6).

His proper attitude toward the honor of people can be seen in Mark 9:25, *"When Jesus saw that the people came running together, He rebuked the foul spirit…."* Instead of waiting for them to come together to see Him cast out the demon, He *"made Himself of no reputation."* He shunned their honor by *not* allowing the crowd to see this miracle of deliverance (see Phil. 2:7). Jesus said, *"I receive not honor from men"* (John 5:41).

In this same Scripture passage (in Matthew), Jesus revealed something very important about overcoming an evil spiritual inheritance. Demons authorized to work through the sins of people's forefathers can be expelled only by prayer and fasting. He said, *"This kind goeth not out but by prayer and fasting"* (Matt. 17:21).

"This kind" refers specifically to demons armed through generational sin. Therefore, in this case, *"this kind"* refers to the deaf and dumb spirit armed through the father's sin of unbelief. The transgression of this boy's father was probably the result of a perverse attitude handed down from previous generations.

Most, if not all of the scriptural examples of repentance of the forefathers' sins and deliverance from the resultant curses involve both prayer and fasting (see Isa. 58:6-12; Neh. 1:3-7; Dan. 9:3-24). *People cannot renounce a generational curse without first repenting of the sins that caused it!* Just saying *"I break this curse"* will not remove it! Curses do not just happen. They are caused by sin. Their cause (root) has to be uncovered and properly dealt with before they are annulled. It takes repentance and confession to remove the stains of sin. People must express heartfelt repentance for the stubborn unbelief and other sins of themselves and their forefathers to obtain complete freedom (see Lev. 26:39-42).

The success of genuine repentance is revealed in Jesus' command to the demon: *"Come out of him, and enter no more into him."* This is the only demon recorded in the Word of God who was forbidden to return after he was cast out! It is also noteworthy that this is the only example in the Gospels where an expelled demon was disarmed before being exorcised (see Mark 9:24-29).

Jesus removed all of the demon's armor. Through His wisdom Jesus took every right that satan had obtained through the stubborn unbelief of the boy's father (see Mark 9:21-23).

The reader should recall that stubbornness is the second defense mechanism introduced in Chapter 13. By stubbornly refusing to hear the advice, warnings, criticisms, and commands of God, parents, and other authorities, people can persist in having their own way. Many people use this protective response to preserve their selfish lifestyles.

So we see that the devil is not the only fool who has resisted God to his own hurt! Because of people's stubborn self-will, satan has many followers. People should realize, however, that their stubborn refusal to hear and obey God also gives satan an avenue to gratify his lusts—through them—at their expense. They should be careful to examine their hearts for all evidence of this perversion if they desire to walk in a way that pleases God.

Next, we will examine how a defiant spirit works to lead people into catering to the next desire of the scorpion. We will also see how this spirit provides the rotational force necessary to continue the advancement of Nature's Wheel.

Sin—Unbelieving

Lust (Eye)—Love of Honor (Praise) of People

Root (Leg)—Self-Will

Branch (Motion)—Stubborn Refusal to Hear

Spirits

Principality (Rule)—Perverse

Power (Authority)—Deaf and Dumb

Might (Miracle Power)—Slothful

Dominion (Mastery)—Defiance

Fruits

Disputations; Heresy; Selfishness; Procrastination;
Performance orientation; Laziness

Some Common Sins in this Category

Arguing; Wastefulness; Proselytizing

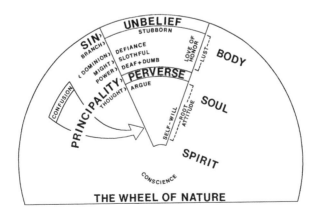

Chapter 15

THE TANGLED WEB

*But the fearful, and unbelieving, and abominable, and murderers, and whoremongers, and sorcerers, and idolaters, and all **liars**, shall have their part in the lake which burneth with fire and brimstone...* (Revelation 21:8).

O
ne of the most amazing incidents recorded in the New Testament concerns the sin of lying. Sudden growth brought the early church into a crisis. Hundreds of people were being saved daily, but many of the new converts were from out of town. The burden of feeding and housing them fell upon the fledgling church. To satisfy the need, the saints began selling property and bringing the money to Peter. In the midst of this revival, a man named Ananias conspired with his wife to deceive the church. This couple sold their land and brought part of the money to Peter, pretending they were offering the full price. They wanted to appear as generous as the other saints without making the same sacrifice. Peter perceived their deception and called their hand:

> *"Ananias, why hath Satan filled thine heart to lie to the Holy Ghost, and to keep back part of the price of the land? Whiles it remained, was it not thine own? And after it was sold, was it not in thine own power? Why hast thou conceived this thing in thine heart? Thou hast not lied unto men, but unto God." And Ananias hearing these words fell down, and gave up the ghost...* (Acts 5:3-5).

Although there is no record of Ananias uttering a single word; yet, he was accused of lying! A lie can be spoken, acted out, or performed simply by keeping quiet, deceiving another person by silence. Regardless of the method used, lying to obtain honor from one's peers is serious sin. The gravity of this sin can be seen in God's swift, deadly judgment upon Ananias and his wife (see Acts 5:7-10).

The human conscience speaks loud and clear when people are about to lie. They must defy their own spirits before they can deceive themselves and others. *One of the fundamental principles of demon activity is that a spirit labors to perform his works both upon and through his victims.* So, a defiant spirit not only resists other people through the one he lives in, he also defies his host's own spirit as well. By resisting the counsel of the human spirit in people, the dominion *spirit of defiance* works to bring them under the influence of the next principality.

Principality (Rule)

This principality, or ruling spirit, is a *lying* spirit. This spirit reasons with people's spirits, convincing and persuading them that it is alright to lie. He struggles to overcome people's natural convictions of right and wrong. The Bible teaches that unless people are convinced that what they are contemplating saying or doing is right, they simply will not yield:

> *All the ways of a man are clean in his own eyes: but the Lord weigheth the spirits. [Also] every way of a man is right in his own eyes: but the Lord pondereth the hearts* (Proverbs 16:2, 21:2).

John's writings reveal the three step process this deception takes:

> *If we say that we have fellowship with Him, and walk in darkness, we lie, and do not the truth...If we say that we have no sin, we deceive ourselves, and the truth is not in us... If we say that we have not sinned, we make Him a liar,* [refute

God's Word and accuse Him of wrong judgment] *and His word is not in us* (1 John 1:6,8,10).

If people pretend to be something they are not, they are walking in darkness, or hypocrisy. Acting out a role instead of being honest brings conviction of wrongdoing from their consciences. They must first defy the counsel of their spirits and then deceive their own hearts before they can perform a deceitful act convincingly (see James 1:22-26).

The root attitude, that something besides the truth is acceptable if it allows people to be or do whatever they please, is *self-deception*. This is the "leg" of the scorpion that satan uses to motivate people to achieve their carnal desires.

The desire in this case is the love of a flawless self-image. This is the "eye" of the scorpion within. The natural fondness that people have to present an impeccable self-image to their peers creates hypocrisy, which Jesus warned against (see Luke 12:1-3):

> *And when thou prayest, thou shalt not be as the hypocrites are: for they love to pray standing in the synagogues and in the corners of the streets, that they may be seen of men...* (Matthew 6:5).

When people crucify the desire for the honor of others, refusing to receive the honor of peers, they are crucifying the world unto themselves (see John 5:41). *Crucifying the love of self-image is crucifying themselves to the world:*

> *But God forbid that I should glory, save in the cross of our Lord Jesus Christ, by whom the world is crucified unto me, and I unto the world* (Galatians 6:14).

Power (Authority)

Once people have accepted the reasoning of a lying spirit in their conscious minds, they are open to a spirit of **divination**. This spirit displaces the human conscience, speaking to people and deceiving them into believing that his thoughts are their thoughts, or even God's. A "familiar spirit" is another common name for this demon (see 1 Sam. 28:7; Acts 16:16-18). This "religious" spirit is the source of much false prophesy and doctrine that the Church has received down through the centuries.

In First Kings 22:6, lying spirits ruled the false prophets of King Ahab. As a result, a spirit of divination had authority to work through them to destroy him. When these false prophets performed before the kings, *they desired to be admired* (see 1 Kings 22:10-12;19-24). Their ambition to present a good image closed their ears so they could not hear the authentic Word of God. Their love of self-image prevented them from being real or true to their own spirits' convictions. In their self-deception, their minds were open to the fraudulent spirits of divination.

When they prophesied, they were not just making things up. They were listening to a spirit of divination. They thought they were actually speaking an oracle of God! This is revealed clearly in both what Micaiah saw (see 1 Kings 22:21-22) and in what Zedekiah said: *"Which way went the Spirit of the Lord from me to speak unto thee?"* (1 Kings 22:24)

Might

Another very important aspect of demonic activity is also revealed in these Scriptures:

> And Zedekiah the son of Chenaanah made him horns of iron: and he said, "Thus saith the Lord, 'With these shalt thou push the Syrians, until thou have consumed them'" (1 Kings 22:11).

This show of power is a manifestation of the spirit of *exhibitionism* working in Zedekiah. This is the might, or power, of satan's forces working through the passions of the false prophet. Exhibitionism is also discernable in the young woman possessed with a spirit of divination in Acts:

142

The same [damsel] *followed Paul and us, and cried, saying, "These men are the servants of the most high God, which shew unto us the way of salvation"* (Acts 16:17).

What she said was true indeed, *but she was false.* She gained attention by associating herself with Paul and his gathering, trying to obtain credibility by pretending to be as they were.

We can see this in our own day as people perform a charade, dropping names and boasting, both in their own, and in their children's, accomplishments. Their motive is to lift themselves up in the eyes of their peers. Their desire is to present a glorious image of themselves.

This is not to say an emotional demonstration cannot be from God. God also heartily exhibits His Word in very expressive ways (see 1 Tim. 4:1). The demonstration of an oracle of God is called a similitude. *A prophet performs a similitude by acting out a prophetic utterance.*

Agabus performed a similitude by binding his own hands and feet with a garment as he prophesied to the apostle Paul (see Acts 21:10-11). Both Ezekiel's and Isaiah's ministries included similitudes (see Isa. 20:2-4; Ezek. 4:1-17, 5:1-4). God said:

> *I have spoken by the prophets, and I have multiplied visions, and used similitudes, by the ministry of the prophets* (Hosea 12:10).

As always, it is not what people do, but what makes them do what they do that counts with God. We must discern who is being glorified to accurately determine the source of the ministry that is being performed (see 1 Cor. 14:29). Jesus said:

> *He that speaketh of himself seeketh his own glory: but he that seeketh His glory that sent him, the same is true, and no unrighteousness is in him* (John 7:18).

A spirit of exhibitionism works to "show off" through his host, glorifying himself in the process. In contrast, Jesus said,

When the Spirit of truth is come, He will guide you into all truth: for He shall not speak of Himself; but…He shall glorify Me: for He shall receive of Mine, and shall shew it unto you (John 16:13-14).

Dominion (Mastery)

The spirit of exhibitionism works in people to act out the counsel of the spirit of divination. As people embrace this their minds come under the delusion and, therefore, the dominion, or mastery, of a spirit of *deception.*

The work of this spirit is to weave a tangled web of deceit to fully dominate his victims. He labors to control people in thought, word, and deed, causing them to deceive themselves and others. Paul spoke of seducers who were continually *"deceiving, and being deceived"* (2 Tim. 3:13). Shakespeare was right when he wrote:

This above all: to thine own self be true,

And it must follow, as the night the day,

Thou canst not then be false to any man.[1]

Some people use deception in an attempt to defend themselves. People use this defense mechanism to hide their faults, inadequacies, insecurities, and feelings of inferiority. In this way they try to project an image of being something that in their hearts they really feel they are not.

This deceptive spirit also uses his host, through worldly wisdom, to con people out of favors, material goods, and even positions of authority. When people have a spirit of deception, they will often attempt to use wisdom to get whatever appears to lift them up and improve their status in this world. The wisdom of satan is expressed with *glorying* and *lying* against the truth.

But if ye have bitter envying and strife in your hearts, glory not, and lie not against the truth. This wisdom descends not from above, but is earthly, sensual, devilish (James 3:14-15).

Satan's first recorded sin on earth was to usurp Adam's authority over God's creation through his cunning craftiness. His purpose was to divert humanity's natural desire to worship God and direct it toward himself. He wanted to steal God's praise and worship for himself. His method was to assume a false role, that of a wise, benevolent counselor. Satan was a liar from the beginning (see Gen. 3:1-5; Isa. 14:12-14; John 8:44).

This is why satan and the spirits that cooperated with him in his error were driven out of God's presence. God cast them down from their former position and the relationship that they had previously enjoyed with Him (see Gen. 3:14; James 3:15; Jude 1:6):

> Ye therefore, beloved, seeing ye know these things before, beware lest ye also, being led away with the error of the wicked, fall from your own steadfastness (2 Peter 3:17).

Believers must refuse satan's attempts to give them a wrong attitude toward the truth. When people refuse to defy their consciences' convictions, they will walk free from this sin. Those who have sinned should pray that God will give them, *"repentance to the acknowledging of the truth"* (2 Tim. 2:25). God's children must recover themselves from the devil's snare.

Like the dominion spirits before him, deception works to entice people to submit to the next principality. For this reason the Wheel of Nature continues its evil progress.

Endnote

1. William Shakespeare, *Hamlet* (1.3.78-80).

Sin—Liars

Lust (Eye)—Love of Self-Image

Root (Leg)—Self-Deception

Branch (Motion)—Hypocrisy

Spirits

Principality (Rule)—Lying

Power (Authority)—Divination

Might (Miracle Power)—Exhibitionism

Dominion (Mastery)—Deception

Fruits

Backbiting; Deceitfulness; Divination (False prophesy);
Exhibitionism; Boasting; Performance orientation

Some Common Sins in this Category:

Conning others out of money; Cheating;
Slander; Gossip; False prophecy

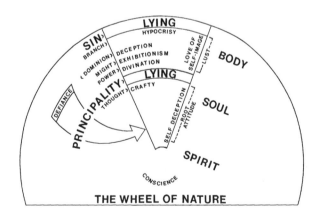

THE WHEEL OF NATURE

Chapter 16

THE DEVIL'S ADVOCATE

*But the fearful, and unbelieving, and **abominable**, [despising] and murderers, and whoremongers, and sorcerers, and idolaters, and all liars, shall have their part in the lake which burneth with fire and brimstone* (Revelation 21:8).

A fascinating paradox is discovered by comparing Revelation 12:7,10 with John 9:31:

> *And there was war in Heaven…and…the accuser of our brethren is cast down, which accused them before our God day and night* (Revelation 12:7,10). [Compared to:] *Now we know God heareth not sinners…* (John 9:31).

If God does not hear sinners, how can satan talk to Him? Of course, we know that when sinners repent and call on the name of Jesus, they have direct access to God (see Acts 2:21,38). But, we also know that, *"the Devil sinneth from the beginning"* (1 John 3:8) and, as we have already seen, he cannot repent. *Therefore, being a sinner, satan has no audience with God* (see 2 Pet. 2:4). Or does he?

How can satan, whom God will not hear, accuse the brethren before God? The answer to this paradox is found in the very same Scripture that creates it:

Now we know that God heareth not sinners: but if any man be a worshipper of God, and doeth His will, him He heareth (John 9:31).

To access God's throne to accuse the brethren, satan must have an advocate. An advocate is one who speaks for another. In this case, the speaker must be a worshiper of God.

To become a Christian, *"we* [had to] *have an advocate with the Father, Jesus Christ the righteous"* (1 John 2:1). Christ had to come before the Father *"to be the propitiation for our sins"* (1 John 4:10) and *"to make intercession for them* [who come unto God by Him]*"* (Heb. 7:25). Likewise, the devil must have someone (a believer) to go before the Lord to plead his case against the brethren. A classic example of satan's accusations against the brethren is found in the book of Job:

Now there was a day when the sons of God came to present themselves before the Lord, and Satan came also among [in or through] *them* (Job 1:6).

Notice here, and also in Job 2:1, that before satan could come into God's presence, he had to be among (in or through) the sons of God. *"Beloved, now are we the sons of God..."* (1 John 3:2). Now, as then, satan uses God's sons and daughters, true believers, to speak for him so that he can accuse the brethren. This is the reason Paul admonished his followers *"to speak evil of no man"* (Tit. 3:2).

The war in (the Kingdom of) Heaven is still being fought! This war will not be won until Christians learn to overthrow the demons which use them as their mouthpieces (see James 3:9-10; Rev. 12:7). When people accuse a brother or sister of wrong-doing, they are allowing satan the use of their tongue to destroy their neighbor. Paul warned:

But if ye bite and devour one another, take heed that ye be not consumed one of another (Galatians 5:15).

Proverbs also warned of the same thing: *"An hypocrite with his mouth destroyeth his neighbor..."* (Prov. 11:9). The mouth of the scorpion within people accuses others of the faults produced by the very same nature of sin they have within themselves. Those who accuse their brothers or sisters *"also are men of like passions"* (Acts 14:15; James 5:17). Jesus said:

> *Judge* [accuse] *not, that ye be not judged. For with what judgment ye judge, ye shall be judged: and with what measure ye mete, it shall be measured to you again. And why beholdest thou the mote* [speck] *that is in thy brother's eye, but considerest not the beam* [foundational problem] *that is in thine own eye? Or how wilt thou say to thy brother, "Let me pull out the mote out of thine eye"; and behold, a beam is in thine own eye? Thou hypocrite, first cast out the beam out of thine own eye; and then shalt thou see clearly to cast out the mote out of thy brothers's eye* (Matthew 7:1-5).

Notice that Jesus was clearly saying that if people accuse another of a fault, the accusers have a greater fault within themselves (see Prov. 10:18). Paul echoed Jesus' words with:

> *Therefore you are inexcusable, O man, whoever you are who judge, for in whatever you judge another you condemn yourself; for you who judge practice the same things* (Romans 2:1 NKJV).

Notice that Paul did not say people condemn themselves *if* they do the same things they accuse their neighbors of; he said the very fact that they were denouncing others meant they either had done or were doing the same things. In other words, the neighbor and the accuser have the same problem!

It is people's own accusations that take away any excuse that they might have had if they had kept silent. They are inexcusable because if they can see that something is wrong in another, they should be able to see that it is wrong within themselves (see John 9:41).

Proverbs 27:19 says, *"As in water face answereth to face, so the heart of man to man."* When people look into a pool of water, they see their own reflection. Likewise, when people look into another person's heart, they see the reflection of their own souls!

An adulterous man does not trust his wife. He sees adulterous desires or motives in her actions, whether her heart is pure or defiled. A thief trusts no one. An unfaithful person thinks all people are untrustworthy.

In the same manner, a fool despises his neighbor, calling him a fool (see Prov. 11:12). A foolish wife does not obey her husband. She thinks he is an idiot. She thinks her wisdom is greater than his and God's, who gave the commandment for the wife to reverence her husband (see Prov. 14:1,21; Eph. 5:22,33).

A gossip accuses her neighbor of talking about others, and the neighbor accuses the gossip of being a talebearer. As long as people accuse and condemn, instead of excusing and justifying, they have the same problem they are seeing in the mirror of their neighbor's heart. Plus, they have the greater fault of accusing another of that which they either have done or are currently doing:

> *Brethren, if a man be overtaken in a fault, ye which are spiritual, restore such an one in the spirit of meekness; considering thyself, lest thou also be tempted* (Galatians 6:1).

Who, then, is spiritual? Paul said in Romans 7:14, "*The law is spiritual....*" He also said that all the Law was fulfilled in this one word, "*... Thou shalt love thy neighbour as thyself. Love worketh no ill to his neighbour: therefore love is the fulfilling of the law*" (Rom. 13:9-10).

Therefore, we can conclude that people who walk in love and who do not condemn, accuse, or harm their neighbor in word or deed are spiritual (see 1 Cor. 10:32). But if people have sin in their hearts, they are not spiritual in that category of sin. James had something to say about this also:

> *Speak not evil one of another, brethren. He that speaketh evil of his brother, and judgeth his brother, speaks evil of the law, and judgeth the law: but if thou judge the law, thou art not a doer of the law, but a judge. There is one lawgiver, who is*

able to save and to destroy: who art thou that judgest another?
(James 4:11-12)

When the Scribes and the Pharisees brought a woman taken in adultery to Jesus, they accused her because they had adultery in their own hearts. Jesus alone did not condemn (accuse) her. When they all left, He asked, *"Woman, where are those thine accusers? Hath no man condemned thee?...Neither do I condemn thee: go, and sin no more"* (see John 8:10-11).

It is only after people have dealt with their own sin nature in the same area as their neighbors' failings that they can perform the delicate task of removing faults from their lives (see 2 Cor. 10:6). Being blinded by self-righteousness will cause people to poke an accusing finger into the eyes of others, justifying themselves as they do.

When people no longer accuse, but instead look beyond their neighbors' faults with compassion and see their needs, they can, indeed, help remove the specks from their eyes (see 2 Thess. 3:14-15). Also, to justify, and thereby excuse their neighbors, is to excuse themselves.

Another aspect of this sin is referred to as grieving the Holy Ghost (or in some cases, even blaspheming!). Proverbs declares that people who are void of wisdom despise their neighbors (see Prov. 11:12). Jesus warned that if people yield to the sin of despising others, they are very close to eternal damnation:

> *But I say unto you that whosoever is angry with his brother without a cause shall be in danger of the judgment; and whosoever shall say to his brother, Raca* [Greek: you are worthless], *shall be in danger of the council: but whosoever shall* [despise his brother and] *say, "Thou fool, shall be in danger of hell fire"* (Matthew 5:22).

Jesus warned of the seriousness of this sin because of a divine principle taught in 1 John 4:20. The way people esteem their brothers and sisters in Christ is the way they regard God. To despise people enough to call others a fool is to despise God and call Him a fool! This is no small trespass.

Hebrews 10:26-31 also warned of the danger of despising God. This is called sinning willfully. *If people despise God in their hearts and sin knowingly and willingly, they blaspheme!* If they blaspheme, they will not be forgiven (see Deut. 29:19-20; Acts 5:1-5).

> *Verily I say unto you, "All sins shall be forgiven unto the sons of men, and blasphemies wherewith soever they shall blaspheme: But he that shall blaspheme against the Holy Ghost hath never forgiveness, but is in danger of eternal damnation." Because they* [despised Him and] *said, "He hath an unclean spirit"* (Mark 3:28-30).

Proverbs 10:18 says, *"...He that utters a slander, is a fool."* Paul's admonition in Ephesians 4:29-32 is more than good advice, it is imperative for eternal life!

> *Let no corrupt communication proceed out of your mouth, but that which is good to the use of edifying, that it may minister grace unto the hearers. And grieve not the holy Spirit of God, whereby ye are sealed unto the day of redemption. Let all bitterness, and wrath, and anger, and clamor, and evil speaking, be put away from you, with all malice: And be ye kind one to another, tenderhearted, forgiving one another, even as God for Christ's sake hath forgiven you* (Ephesians 4:29-32).

Principality (Rule)

As I have mentioned before, when satan tempts people, he must first convince them that they are just in their cause before they will sin. A spirit of deception works to convince people that they are justified in their actions. Through this evil spirit's cunning deceitfulness, people esteem themselves right in their own judgments.

All the ways of a man are clean in his own eyes: but the Lord weigheth the spirits....Every way of a man is right in his own eyes... (Proverbs 16:2; 21:2).

Proverbs 12:15 also says, *"The way of a fool is right in his own eyes...."* Once this wicked spirit has succeeded in putting an attitude of self-justification into people's hearts, the principality of **haughtiness** will cause them to despise others (see Prov. 11:12, 12:15).

All people are of like passions, and consequently, everyone must overcome the same temptations. Even Jesus was tempted in all points like as we are (see Luke 22:28; Heb. 4:15). But when people have truly overcome their sin nature, they will have compassion on others instead of condemning them because they will understand them. They will sympathize with those still wrestling in their minds and emotions with the principalities and powers over which God has graciously given them victory (see Eph. 6:12).

When people despise and accuse others, they have the accuser of the brethren within themselves! They have justified themselves, but they see the reflection of their own sinful condition in their neighbors' hearts, and they don't like what they see! By accusing others, they destroy themselves: *"For by thy words thou shalt be justified, and by thy words thou shalt be condemned"* (Matt. 12:37).

Their own spirits recognize that they are wrong. But in their carnal minds, through the influence of the spirit of haughtiness, they feel justified in their accusations. They have silenced their own spirits with self-justification because of their desire to esteem themselves as righteous, or right. This self-righteous desire to esteem themselves above others is the "eye" of the scorpion within people. The desire to justify themselves, or self-justification, is the "leg" of the scorpion.

If people would properly judge themselves, they would not condemn others. Paul taught that people are a law unto themselves, their consciences truthfully bearing witness of their sinfulness or of their righteousness. If people are righteous, they will justify and excuse others. But if they are self-righteous, they will accuse and denounce others in their haughtiness (see Rom. 2:14-15).

Power (Authority)

The influence of the spirit of haughtiness allows the spirit of **blindness** to close the eyes of people's understanding. Then they cannot see themselves as they really are because they are blinded to their own true state (see Prov. 16:18; Matt. 12:22; 2 Cor. 4:4). Once people have submitted to the authority of this spirit, they are moved to criticize others. They despise those who are not walking in the righteousness or goodness that they think they are personally walking in.

It is this self-righteous criticism of others that is behind much of the contention and strife that is in the churches. No other area of people's personality, or soul, lends itself so well to the development of the leaven of the Pharisees than this area. Jesus warned His followers to beware of this evil doctrine (manner of thinking) several different times:

> *Then Jesus said unto them, "Take heed and beware of the leaven of the Pharisees and of the Sadducees...." Then understood they how that He bade them not beware of the leaven of bread, but of the doctrine of the Pharisees and of the Sadducees* (Matthew 16:6,12).

> *And He spake...unto* [the Pharisees] *which trusted in themselves that they were righteous, and despised others..."Ye* [Pharisees]... *justify yourselves before men; but God knoweth your hearts: for that which is highly esteemed among men is an abomination in the sight of God"* (Luke 18:9, 16:15).

Brothers scorn brothers; sisters despise sisters. Elders call God's sheep *"goats,"* and the sheep butt the elders. Separating themselves either into denominations (those who name themselves) or nondenominations, today's Christians repeat the error of the Corinthians (see 1 Cor. 3:3-6).

Being carnal, they compete for souls like football players competing for points.

Their self-justifications are varied and many. Many speak of justification by faith, but their faith is directed toward their pet doctrines, not Christ. Some center themselves around different forms of church government—thus, they name themselves. Others gather around different ordinances, such as communion or baptism, and some around different ways of administering the ordinances. Others see unconventional forms of worship as a reason to despise their brethren. Dancing, lifting of the hands, or playing instruments of music become the focus of their faith or of their criticism.

> *Shall the sword devour forever, knowest thou not that it will be bitterness in the latter end? How long shall it be then, ere thou bid the people return from following their brethren?* (2 Samuel 2:26)

It makes no difference whether a Christian's faith is in his form of church government or in the way he observes certain ordinances, it will avail nothing if it is not in Christ. Communion, baptism (either water or spirit), speaking in tongues or not speaking in tongues, lifting hands or not lifting hands, none of these—nor anything else other than faith in Christ—is supposed to be the basis for fellowship and unity (see Matt. 16:16-18; 1 John 1:6-7, 3:14, 4:20-21).

Regardless if people's faith is in their holiness standards or in their liberty from religious legalism, they are still carnal and their faith is misdirected. Instead of producing love, such *"faith"* will cause strife and division (see John 16:2). Paul admonished his followers to continually *"endeavouring to keep the unity of the spirit in the bond of peace...until we all come in the unity of the faith..."* (Eph. 4:3,13). The Church needs a visitation from God like Job's. It was not until God dealt with Job's self-righteous attitude that his eyes were opened:

> *So these three men ceased to answer Job, because he was righteous in his own eyes. Then was kindled the wrath of Elihu...*

against Job was his wrath kindled, because he justified himself rather than God (Job 32:1-2).

God's rebuke, through Elihu, was to both Job and to his friends—*they were all wrong.* After God reproved them all, Job saw his self-righteousness for the first time:

I have heard of Thee by the hearing of the ear: but now mine eye seeth Thee. Wherefore I abhor myself, and I repent in dust and ashes (Job 42:5-6).

When Job repented, blindness was no longer able to close his eyes. God opened the eyes of his understanding, and for the first time he actually saw himself the way he really was.

Let's pray for God to open the eyes of our understanding, too! Instead of accusing one another, Christians should pray for those they *think* may be wrong or deceived (see Eph. 1:16-18). God delivered Job from his captivity when he prayed for the friends who accused him (see Job 42:10; 3 John 14). *It is time for the Church to repent!*

Might

As a result of this blindness, the powerful spirit of **criticism** works in many Christians to scorn others. Many of those who are judged as not being holy, spiritual, wise, wealthy, beautiful, hard working, or whatever vanity people are deceived by—are despised. This scornful anger directed toward others brings forth God's wrath upon the people who are judging because they are condemned by their own accusations (see Prov. 19:19; 2 Sam. 12:5-12; Matt. 7:1-2; Rom. 1:18, 2:1-5).

The accusers' hearts know the real truth, and their consciences cry out to them, charging them with sin. If they acknowledge that voice, they are convicted of sin and repent—unless they are carnal minded—then they will not repent because of pride.

Dominion (Mastery)

To avoid humbling themselves and repenting, people defend themselves by accusing and criticizing others. Their *"righteous indignation"* opens the way for a spirit of **strife** to work:

> *Proud and haughty scorner is his name, who dealeth in proud wrath* (Proverbs 21:24).

Self-righteous indignation does not work righteousness; it only destroys the one who is self-righteous, *"For the wrath of man worketh not the righteousness of God"* (James 1:20).

It was the sin of despising others, and the strife that it spawns, that Jesus searched for as He gave His disciples their final examination. Previously, He had charged them with, *"Have not I chosen you twelve, and one of you is a devil?"* (John 6:70) Then, gathering them together at the last supper, He said:

> *"Verily I say unto you, that one of you shall betray Me." And they were exceeding sorrowful, and began every one of them to say unto Him, "Lord, is it I?"* (Matthew 26:21-22)

In this final examination, Jesus searched their hearts for any evidence of the accuser of the brethren dwelling there. If their hearts had not been cleansed by His Word, they probably would have accused one another (see John 15:3). One or more of them would have smirked and pointed to a fellow disciple with, *"Yes, and I know who it is, too!"* or a similar accusation or criticism. Possibly some would have blamed Peter; after all, had not Jesus called him *"satan"* earlier in their training? (See Matthew 16:23.)

But instead of accusing each other, their earnest question, *"Lord, is it I?"* revealed the soul-searching that was going on in their hearts. This was the answer of a good conscience that Jesus was looking for. To have received any other response would have told Him that His work was not finished. It had been only a few hours since He had given them their last training lesson:

And it came to pass, when the time was come that He should be received up, He steadfastly set His face to go to Jerusalem, and sent messengers before His face: and they went, and entered into a village of the Samaritans, to make ready for Him. And they did not receive Him, because His face was as though He would go to Jerusalem. And when His disciples James and John saw this, they said, "Lord wilt Thou that we command fire to come down from heaven, and consume them as Elias did?" But He turned, and rebuked them, and said, "Ye know not what manner of spirit ye are of. For the Son of man is not come to destroy men's lives, but to save them..." (Luke 9:51-56).

After pointing out His disciples' error, Jesus, as always, followed His rebuke with corrective instructions. Like Paul (in his letter to the Philippians), Jesus refused to allow contention to dissuade Him from fulfilling His Master's instructions. He never deviated from the job He was sent to accomplish—to save the lost (see Phil. 1:15-18).

To correct His disciples' contentious manner of spirit, He gave them several parables. Today's Christians will do well to observe these same corrections. The first one was:

And it came to pass, that as they went in the way, a certain man said unto Him, "Lord, I will follow Thee whithersoever Thou goest." And Jesus said unto him, "Foxes have holes, and birds of the air have nests; but the Son of man hath not where to lay His head" (Luke 9:57-58).

Paul revealed the meaning of this parable in his letter to the Philippians:

Let nothing be done through strife or vainglory; but in lowliness of mind let each esteem other better than themselves. Look not every man on his own things, but every man on the things of others...for the work of Christ he [Epaphroditus] *was nigh unto death, not regarding his life, to supply your lack of service toward me* (Philippians 2:3-4,30).

158

Both Jesus and Paul refused to allow contention concerning natural things to enter their hearts. Epaphroditus served Jesus by serving Paul. He did not allow anything to sway him from his assigned mission. Even the threat of death could not stop him.

It was contention over worldly possessions that separated the father of faith, Abraham, from his nephew Lot. Although God ordained people to use this world, they must not abuse this privilege. They cannot allow strife over *"things"* into their hearts (see Gen. 13:2-9; 1 Cor. 7:30-31). God requires His children to walk in *"lowliness of mind"* (Phil. 2:3). Proverbs 13:10 is very emphatic: ***"Only*** *by pride cometh contention...."* The second correction Jesus gave His disciples was:

> *And He said unto another, "Follow Me." But he said, "Lord, suffer me first to go and bury my father." Jesus said unto him, "Let the dead bury their dead; but go thou and preach the kingdom of God"* (Luke 9:59-60).

To fully understand this parable, we should realize that this man's father was still alive. In essence, he was saying that after his father died and he received his inheritance, then he would serve Jesus. His heart was not with the Lord, but rather on possessions and positions in the world. Paul addressed this wrong manner of thinking in Philippians 3:

> *If any other man thinketh that he hath whereof he might trust in the flesh, I more...But what things were gain to me, those I counted loss for Christ. Yea doubtless, and I count all things but loss for the excellency of the knowledge of Christ Jesus my Lord: For whom I have suffered the loss of all things, and do count them but dung, that I may win Christ...* (Philippians 3:4, 7-8).

After this admonition, Jesus gave the third parable of correction:

> *And another also said, "Lord, I will follow Thee; but let me first go bid them farewell, which are at home at my house." And Jesus said unto him, "No man, having put his hand to the*

plough, and looking back, is fit for the kingdom of God" (Luke 9:61-62).

Again, Paul interpreted this parable in Philippians 3:

> *Brethren, I count not myself to have apprehended: but this one thing I do, forgetting those things which are behind, and reaching forth unto those things which are before, I press toward the mark for the prize of the high calling of God in Christ Jesus. Let us therefore, as many as be perfect* [mature], *be thus minded...* (Philippians 3:13-15).

Whether people glance back with regrets over their own faults, past failures, or losses, or whether they glare back with offense over the wrongs done to them by others—it is the same. They cannot afford to allow the past to destroy their present blessings or the future hope they have in Christ. They cannot apprehend (grasp) all that God has purchased for them through the cross if they refuse to release the past. Later, we will see that remembering the past is what opens people's hearts to the influence of the next principality.

In summary, we have seen how a wrong attitude developed through a *spirit of deception* causes people to justify themselves in their hearts while at the same time accusing others. Esteeming themselves better than their neighbors, they walk with a *haughty spirit,* despising others in their *blindness.* They cannot see their own weaknesses and faults. Being scornfully *critical* of others, their hearts are open to contentious, wrathful *strife.* This demon works through their *self-"righteous indignation"* to destroy both his hosts and those his hosts accuse (see Prov. 26:20-21, 28:25):

> *Pride goeth before destruction, and an haughty spirit before a fall* (Proverbs 16:18).

A haughty spirit working through the pride of life causes people to trip themselves with their own words. Snared with the words of their own judgments, they destroy themselves (see Prov. 12:13).

As people yield their members to the dominion of the spirit of strife, this demon obtains mastery over his victims' minds to pave the way for the next principality. This empowers the Wheel of Nature to continue its incessant progress (see Prov. 27:4):

> *And the tongue is a fire. [The tongue is a] world of wicked-*
> *ness set among our members, contaminating and depraving the*
> *whole body and setting on fire the **wheel of... nature**—being*
> *itself ignited by hell...* (James 3:6 AMP).

Only knowing and remembering that all people are of like passions will save Christians from the devastation brought about by accusing words (see 2 Pet. 1:9). When people hear and obey the cleansing Word of God and learn to *"love mercy and not sacrifice"* (Matt. 12:7), they will not despise God or their neighbors. The importance of this cleansing is seen in Revelation 12:10:

> *And I heard a loud voice saying in heaven, "Now is come sal-*
> *vation, and strength, and the kingdom of our God, and the*
> *power of His Christ: for the accuser of our brethren is cast*
> *down, which accused them before our God day and night"*
> (Revelation 12:10).

Some believers think that the war spoken of here occurred before the Garden of Eden, while others think it occurred when Jesus ascended into Heaven. Look closely and notice that the result of this war is the saints' ultimate victory over the devil. This certainly has not happened! John said that his prophesies were still in the future at the time of his writing (see Rev. 1:19, 4:1). Experience says that this war is still in progress.

This battle is still before the Church; this victory is yet to be won. The Kingdom of Heaven suffers violence, but Jesus has assured His followers that the gates of hell will not prevail (see Matt. 11:12, 16:18). To win this war the Church must, *"Cast out the scorner, and contention shall go out; yea strife and reproach shall cease"* (Prov. 22:10). Amen.

Sin—Despising

Lust (Eye)—Love of Self-Esteem

Root (Leg)—Self-Justification

Branch (Motion)—Self-Righteousness

Spirits

Principality (Rule)—Haughty

Power (Authority)—Blindness

Might (Miracle Power)—Critical

Dominion (Mastery)—Strife

Fruits

Arrogance; Pride; Mocking; Scoffing; Contention;
Critical disposition; Prejudice

Some Common Sins in this Category:

Hostile to virtue; Accuser of others;
Scornfulness; Strife; Racism; Slander

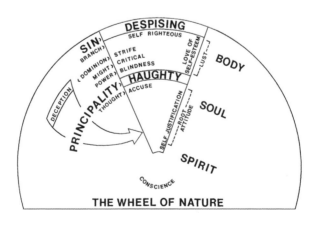

THE WHEEL OF NATURE

Chapter 17

THE BITTERNESS OF DEATH

But the fearful, and unbelieving, and the abominable, and **murderers***, and whoremongers, and sorcerers, and idolaters, and all liars, shall have their part in the lake which burneth with fire and brimstone...* (Revelation 21:8).

As we continue our investigation of the scorpion, we come to the normal results of the dominion of strife working in people's lives. No other segment of the sin nature crushes the joy and spontaneity out of life as this one does. Strife produces offense. Offense quickly grows into hatred. Hatred, like an acid, does more harm to the vessel in which it is stored than the person upon whom it is poured.

All people are subject to the spirit of strife and the offenses which follow because of the deceitful passions and lusts that work in their members. The inevitable result of offense is hatred. Hatred is murder. John said, *"Whosoever hateth his brother is a murderer"* (1 John 3:15).

Examining strife in the Bible, we see that God's very first family quickly fell into strife. After Adam disobeyed God, he accused his wife and God for his own error in judgment and the sin that he committed. Then Adam's sons carried on the family quarrel until it ended in murder. *Cain killed Able in a religious dispute* (see Gen. 3:12, 4:3-8).

Abraham's family also struggled with strife. Abraham and his nephew Lot were separated by conflict over their abundant wealth. He also reproved Abimelech over a well of water that Abimelech's servants had violently taken away from him. Likewise, Abraham's wife got into strife. Sarah strove with her handmaid over their two sons. She was determined that her son Isaac would inherit the promises given to Abraham and not Ishmael (see Gen. 13:2,5-9, 14:8-16, 21:9-12,25).

Another interesting incidence of strife recorded in the Scriptures involved two of God's chief apostles. In Antioch, Paul and Barnabas contended with the Pharisees concerning whether the Gentile Christians should keep the Mosaic Law. When they were unable to resolve this issue among themselves, they presented the problem to the apostles at Jerusalem.

At the council in Jerusalem there was much disputing over this issue. After listening to both sides of the debate, James reached a decision and passed sentence on the question. Because his verdict was in favor of the position Paul and Barnabas had taken, they won a decisive victory over their opponents.

But the strife did not end there. The two apostles began to strive between themselves over whether Mark was to go with them on their next missionary journey. The friction between these two chief men became so great that it splintered their relationship and separated them (see Acts 15:1-2;5-20;36-40).

Jesus warned, *"Woe unto the world because of offenses..."* (Matt. 18:7). The primary *"woes"* of this world occur because people offend one another. Whether they offend or are offended, they suffer (see Eccl. 4:1).

Although thoughtless people are a major source of offense, occasionally offenses come through natural or personal disasters. However, sometimes natural disasters also serve to bring out the best in people (see Rom. 8:28). In place of heartaches, they may leave blessings, especially when those who are troubled receive help from others. It is not unusual for assistance from compassionate strangers or friendly neighbors to restore people's faith in God and humanity (see 2 Cor. 9:12-13).

In the process of time, the trauma experienced through the destruction of a storm, earthquake, or house fire is overcome and forgotten while the fond memories of kind strangers and helpful neighbors remain. On the other hand, children never forget the trauma caused by an offensive parent's harsh abuse unless they are healed through forgiveness.

Crimes against people or possessions, such as rape, robbery, adultery, unfaithfulness, or betrayal are seldom forgotten. This is especially true if the offense comes from a close friend or loved one. Regardless of the source, these wounds usually leave indelible scars that time will not erase.

Only God's love, working through and upon people, is able to repair these damages. The cross alone can restore people to mental, emotional, and sometimes even physical health when they have suffered severe heartaches (see 1 Cor. 1:18).

Likewise, those who cause such offenses need God's help. Only the blood of our Lord Jesus can cleanse people's tormented consciences when they carry a load of guilt. When people have offended and wounded others, they must wash themselves with repentance and confession to cleanse their consciences. Confessing their sins is the only thing that will remove the condemnation of being the perpetrator of pain and heartache upon others (see Ps. 51:1-10; Heb. 9:14).

Strife is one of the chief sources of offense, and through strife people are exposed to another of satan's evil workers of darkness—*envy*. James asked:

> *From whence come wars and fightings among you? Come they not hence, even of your lusts that war in your members?... Do ye think that the Scripture saith in vain, "The spirit that dwelleth in us lusteth to* [or for] *envy?"* (James 4:1,5)

James was speaking here of the natural desire people have to be envied by their neighbors. (A car salesman draws on this natural instinct when he tells his prospective client, *"If you buy this car, your neighbors will be green with envy!"*) This natural tendency to desire the envy of others opens people's hearts to an *unclean spirit of envy*, which works through the spirit of the carnal mind. James makes this abundantly clear in the surrounding verses: *"This wisdom descendeth not from above, but is earthly, sensual, devilish"* (James 3:15), and *"Resist the Devil, and he will flee from you"* (James 4:7-8).

If we continue reading, James declares the same truth we have previously learned—through a haughty, accusing spirit, people bring strife and bitterness into their own lives by yielding their minds to the enemy of their souls (see James 4:1-12). James also warned:

> *If ye have bitter envying and strife in your hearts, glory not, and lie not against the truth* (James 3:14).

When people are offended, they resent both the offense and those whom they think perpetrated the injustice. If people do not hold the truth in their hearts, they will falsely or unjustly accuse those whom they dislike. Therefore, James warned Christians of the subtle danger of lying about others because they are offended at them.

Solomon also taught about lying and resentment: *"A lying tongue hateth those that are afflicted by it..."* (Prov. 26:28). When people are envious or jealous, they desire to accuse (murder with words) those by whom they feel threatened. Therefore, they will receive false accusations against anyone whom they envy. They will also aid in spreading lies about those toward whom they are bitter (see Matt. 26:59-62, 27:18):

> *Follow peace with all men...Looking diligently lest any man fail of the grace of God; lest any root of bitterness springing up trouble you, and thereby many be defiled* (Hebrews 12:14-15).

> *Let all bitterness, and wrath, and anger, and clamour, and evil speaking* [slander], *be put away from you, with all malice: And be ye kind one to another, tenderhearted, forgiving one another, even as God for Christ's sake hath forgiven you* (Ephesians 4:31-32).

The only way to keep the heart free from bitter envy is to forgive *every* offense. Jesus said, *"And when ye stand praying, forgive, if ye have ought against any"* (Mark 11:25). *"Ought"* is a *very* small amount! When people refuse to forgive others (whether their trespasses are real or imagined), they are defiled, and they destroy themselves. Jesus, in His instructions on how to pray, said *"Forgive us our debts, as we forgive our debtors"* (Matt. 6:12). When He further expounded on this prayer, He said:

> *For if ye forgive men their trespasses, your heavenly Father will also forgive you: But if ye forgive not men their trespasses, neither will your Father forgive your trespasses* (Matthew 6:14-15).

In these Scriptures Jesus equated *"debts"* and *"trespasses"* (understanding this helps people forgive). When people are offended, they unconsciously feel that the wrongdoer owes them a just recompense. *Thus, a trespass creates a debt.* If they do not receive what they feel is a just payment, their memories add this debt to the wrongdoer's account. They will retain it in their memories until it is either repaid or forgiven.

If it is not forgiven, and the offender does not recompense them for the injustice that they suffered, they feel that whatever the debtor has should be theirs. This may be material goods, peace, reputation, happiness, pleasure, or anything else the debtor may have. In their opinion, whatever the wrongdoer has is really theirs. When people desire to have what is in another's possession because they feel it really belongs to them, the emotion they experience is called bitter envying.

This resentment, or bitterness, activates the inherent desire for revenge, to which all people are susceptible. Bitterness, or bitter envying, is the motivating "leg" of the scorpion which works in people to activate their natural desire to "get even." Both the Old and New Testaments forbid God's children from seeking revenge.

> *Thou shalt not avenge, nor bear any grudge against the children of thy people, but thou shalt love thy neighbor as thyself* (Leviticus 19:18).

Dearly beloved, avenge not yourselves, but rather give place unto wrath: for it is written, "Vengeance is Mine; I will repay," saith the Lord (Romans 12:19).

The desire for revenge has two parts—*recompense* (to get back that which is loss) and *retaliation* (to inflict pain and suffering upon others as punishment for what they have done). Or, as the golden rule has so often been misquoted as saying, the desire is to, *"Do unto others as they have done unto you."* Understanding both parts of the desire for revenge is tremendously helpful when people are trying to forgive someone of wrongdoing.

When people suffer injury or abuse, they desire to reclaim their loss. Because they feel that whatever they lost was rightfully their own, they feel they have a right to get it back. This desire for recompense is the same as envy. To desire what another person has is envy.

Assume, for example, that a man is in line for a promotion. Even if the promotion is not actually earned, if he thinks he is qualified for it, he may feel that it is rightfully his. Then, if another employee receives this advancement instead, if the man is carnal minded, he will feel envy toward the promoted person. In his heart he believes that his fellow employee took his position. He feels that his employer gave away something that belonged to him. Often, he will be bitter toward both his fellow employee and his boss.

Another example is the envy people feel when another person obtains something better than what they have. People often resent the rich just falling into opportunity and good fortune (or so it seems) while they themselves have to work for every dime! Of course, this is rightly called *class envy*.

No one is immune to the influence of the spirit of envy. Even King David, who was a man after God's own heart, confessed:

But as for me, my feet were almost gone; my steps had well nigh slipped. For I was envious at the foolish, when I saw the prosperity of the wicked. For there are no bands in their death:

but their strength is firm. They are not in trouble as other men; neither are they plagued like other men. Therefore pride compasseth them about as a chain; violence covereth them as a garment. Their eyes stand out with fatness: they have more than heart could wish (Psalm 73:2-7).

When people are carnal minded and they see others blessed, they feel they should have a right to the same blessings. Inwardly, they resent the more fortunate person's prosperity. They think the fame, fortune, favor, or whatever else the other person received, somehow, should be theirs.

This is especially true if at one time it *was* theirs. Jesus taught people to give up all their rights and to leave their peace, prosperity, and pleasure in His hands. To avoid giving place to envy, Jesus said that when someone takes our coat we should also give that person our cloak. When someone slaps one cheek, we should turn the other (see Matt. 5:38-41).

Christians are to forgive and bless the people who misuse and abuse them. They should pray for the salvation of those who offend them and then do something good for them as occasion permits (see Matt. 5:44; Acts 3:26). This is particularly true concerning parents. Even when a parent has denied children what could be considered a normal childhood or upbringing, the children should honor the parents anyway. It is utterly necessary to forgive parents of all wrongs and shortcomings in order to have the fullness of God's blessings:

Honour thy father and mother; which is the first commandment with promise; that it may be well with thee, and thou mayest live long on the earth (Ephesians 6:2-3).

People cannot honor their father and mother and at the same time hold grievances toward them in their hearts. When children forgive their parents, the way is opened for their own trespasses to be forgiven. There are no perfect parents, but there are no perfect children either! People must both forgive and be forgiven. Giving mercy to parents will also help free people from perpetrating the same hurts upon their own children (see Hos. 10:12).

If people do not forgive, they will feel that they have a right to all that they have lost. They will even desire harm upon those who mistreated them. This desire for their harm, or the urge to *"get even"* with the people that have offended them, is often unconscious—especially when it is directed toward those who are or should be loved (see Acts 7:9, 13:44-45, 17:5).

For example, if a husband commits adultery, the offended wife believes that she deserves repayment. To collect this debt, she may commit adultery in retaliation or resort to hurting her husband with words, denial of companionship, or other diverse ways. Either way, she feels justified in her thoughts, words, and actions because of the debt she is collecting.

Christians should realize that all behavior that is not under the Universal Law of Love, including lustful thought, is sin. Offended Christians must reevaluate their self-justifying attitudes and vengeful acts. "Two wrongs do not make a right." For instance, everyone is subject to temptation through lustful thinking, and sooner or later, everyone succumbs to adultery in his or her own thoughts. Forgiving a spouse of adultery allows God to forgive you of your own adulteries, whether they were in thought, word, or deed. Refusing to forgive brings God's righteous judgment down upon you (see Matt. 5:27-28; Rom. 2:1-6).

Perhaps the hardest trespass to forgive is when love is given and evil is received in return. It is difficult for people to forgive trusted friends or family members whom they have helped, cared for, and freely loved when they, in turn, betray the one who loved them. The debt they owe is love. They must give *them* the love *they owe* without desiring recompense or retaliation (see Ps. 41:9; John 13:1,18). As with all other debts, people should freely release others from all trespasses.

The ways people offend and become offended are many. When offended, the insidious desire for revenge is the "eye" of the scorpion activated within people (see Lev. 19:17-18).

Principality (Rule)

Strife unchecked and its many wounds unhealed expose people's minds to the influence of the next principality of satan. This is the wicked spirit of *envy*.

> *Wrath is cruel, and anger is outrageous; but who is able to stand before envy?* (Proverbs 27:4)

The chief priests delivered Jesus to Pilate to be crucified (murdered) because of envy (see Mark 15:10). The religious leaders felt that the people following Jesus should be following them because they fasted and Jesus' disciples did not. They resented Jesus and accused Him of being a deceiver. They reasoned that if God was going to work in miraculous ways it should be through them. They thought God was in error if He performed miracles through Jesus! He would not even obey *their* laws (see Mark 2:18; John 7:12, 9:16,24, 12:19).

Power (Authority)

When the principality of envy persuades people that others have treated them unfairly, the insidious desire for revenge is activated. As a result, the offended people become hardhearted toward their offenders. Because they have bitterness in their hearts, they will resist the prompting of their consciences to forgive the transgression.

When people do not forgive, an ***unforgiving*** spirit is authorized to work within them. This spirit works through their carnal minds and imaginations to keep them in a continual state of bitterness.

When people yield to the carnal desire for revenge, they receive evil thoughts injected into their conscious minds. When people can consciously remember the injustices they have suffered, it is often hard to resist brooding over the grievances they carry. An unforgiving spirit will keep bringing the painful thoughts and imaginations back again and again.

There are times when a particular offense is so painful that certain people (especially young children) will block it from their conscious memory. This, however, does not remove it from the subconscious, or carnal mind.

Even when people cannot consciously remember an offense, they will still struggle within their emotions and have bitter feelings toward certain people. Bitter, subconscious memories make people react through conditioned responses in either offensive or defensive ways. These sensations and responses leave people feeling guilty and resentful without always being able to understand why.

Might

When people harbor unforgiven grievances in their hearts, the powerful spirit of *jealousy* is able to bring his destructive forces into work through their passions. Jealousy activates the emotions of fear and hatred in his victims' hearts (see Num. 5:14).

As we have learned, when people have suffered loss, a debt is created. Jealousy causes them to fear that they will not receive repayment. The spirit of jealousy also causes people to be apprehensive concerning losing things they already have. This evil spirit makes his victims offended toward anyone they think may interfere with their relationships or take away their possessions (see Luke 15:27-28).

Jealousy causes people to distrust others, making them apprehensive and angry, thereby robbing them of peace. *Jealousy expresses himself through two of humanity's strongest emotions, fear and hatred.* Both of these emotions are very powerful. Together they account for one of the best known expressions of this evil spirit—rage:

> *For jealousy is the rage of a man: therefore he will not spare in the day of vengeance...neither will he rest content...* (Proverbs 6:34-35).

Dominion (Mastery)

Just as unforgiven offenses open people's hearts to a spirit of jealousy, jealousy in turn stimulates the offended people to hate the wrongdoers. The spirit of **hatred** then brings forth thoughts of revenge and plots different ways and means of getting even (see Ezek. 25:15). Although, they may not actually kill those they hate, as we have already seen, John said that to hate another person is murder (see 1 John 3:15).

As we saw in the Scripture quoted on the previous page, the rage of jealousy provides the emotional force necessary to carry out the desires of the spirit of hate: *"For jealousy is the rage of a man: therefore he will not spare in the day of vengeance"* (Prov. 6:34).

The wicked spirit of hatred will even cause people to betray their own family and friends. This evil manifestation of the destroyer divides and wrecks families, friendships, and marriages. He strives to actually kill people when he is in full control. When he cannot kill with guns or knives, he uses accusing, harsh, and (often) lying words (see Jer. 18:18; John 8:44). Be not deceived! A Christian cannot hate anyone and still be saved: *"Whosoever hates his brother is a murderer: and ye know that no murderer has eternal life abiding in him"* (Mal. 2:10; Matt. 5:21-24, 6:15; Mark 11:25-26; 1 John 3:12-15).

In Matthew 18:23-35, Jesus told a parable of two servants with unpayable debts. This story reveals the necessity of being merciful and forgiving toward others. Christians should love others regardless of any violation of their own rights. *This parable also teaches how to forgive!*

In this story, a certain servant was called into account for his debt. When confronted, he asked for time to be able to raise the amount owed. But his Lord just forgave him instead. Then this same man went to one of his fellow servants and called him into account for a debt. His fellow servant likewise asked for additional time to make good on his debt.

Since the first servant received forgiveness, he had mercy to share with his fellow servant. Instead of being merciful, he refused to release his companion and demanded immediate payment. When the report of his actions reached his master, the Scripture records:

> *Then his master, after he called him, said to him, "You wicked servant! I forgave you all that debt because you begged me. Should you not also have had compassion on your fellow servant, just as I had pity on you?" And his master was angry, and delivered him to the torturers until he should pay all that was due to him. So My heavenly Father also will do to you if each of you, from his heart, does not forgive his brother his trespasses* (Matthew 18:32-35 NKJV).

God does not expect anyone to forgive unless he first receives forgiveness. Nor are people able, as they cannot give something they do not have. Until they receive mercy and are forgiven, they have no mercy to give. Therefore, the way to forgive others is for people to first confess their own sin and by faith receive God's mercy and forgiveness.

When people accuse others and justify themselves, they cannot forgive. They must first acknowledge and confess their own part in the injustices they have suffered before they can forgive. If they do not, they cannot escape the bitterness they feel, even when they desire to forgive and say they forgive.

When people are truly innocent of any wrongdoing in a specific offense, but they feel offended anyway, their sin is the grudge that they harbor in their hearts. A grudge is a sin—a sin that God must forgive before people can release their offenders (see Lev. 19:17-18; James 5:9). *A grudge is long-term anger caused by an offense.* The Bible gives the time limit for anger before it becomes a grudge:

> *Be ye angry and sin not: let not the sun go down upon your wrath* (Ephesians 4:26).

The Word of God commands people to deal properly with anger and wrath *on the same day the offense occurs.* If they do not, they are guilty of the sin of carrying a grudge.

THE BITTERNESS OF DEATH

Seven Steps to Forgive

There are seven, distinct steps, involving seven, specific issues, that people must deal with before forgiveness is effective. When applicable, each of the seven steps should be observed.

Participation—Acknowledge and confess as sin your own participation in the wrong which has been committed.

Grudge—Confess as sin your own offence and negative reaction to the trespass.

Recompense—Analyze and forgive the debt. This releases you from the desire for recompense (grief).

Retaliation—Justify and pray for your debtors. This overcomes the desire for retaliation (anger).

Appeal—When the offense is ongoing, appeal to the higher authority (pray for God to judge the offender).

Faith—Receive God's forgiveness for yourself.

Self-forgiveness—Self-forgiveness is necessary before you can obtain freedom from self-hatred, guilt, hurt, pride, etc. It is also necessary before complete emotional *healing* will be obtained.

In summary, we can see that when people choose to deny the counsel of their own spirits and the commands of God's Word, they fall into a deadly snare. To refuse to forgive all who have wronged them is spiritual suicide (see Matt. 6:15, 18:34-35).

Through bitter feelings, the spirit of *envy* persuades people that it is alright not to forgive those who have violated their rights. Instead of compassion, the spirit of envy arouses the desire for recompense, to get back all they have lost. Depression is inevitable for these people as they continually wallow in grief and self-pity.

An *unforgiving* spirit causes grudge-holders to brood (consciously or unconsciously) on the unfairness of their situations. This spirit resists all thoughts of love and mercy and continuously injects brooding reminders of any injustices they have suffered into their conscious minds.

The spirit of *jealousy* torments his victims with fear. He also arouses passions of rage toward the people who offended and injured his hosts. Then the spirit of *hatred* dominates people's minds to speak and act against those who wronged them. This spirit causes people to desire harm upon those perceived as their enemies and betrayers (although they are not always consciously perceived as enemies). When offences remain, anger will continually boil up and spill over, contaminating other relationships and areas of their lives. These evil passions empower the Wheel of Nature as it continues its roll.

Sin—Murder

Lust (Eye)—Love of Revenge

Root (Leg)—Bitterness

Branch (Motion)—Hatred

Spirits

Principality (Rule)—Envy

Power (Authority)—Unforgiving

Might (Miracle Power)—Jealousy

Dominion (Mastery)—Hate

Fruits

Plotting evil; Bad memories; Brooding over injustices

Some Common Sins in this Category:

Grudging; Cruelty; Unmerciful; Betrayal; Malicious lies

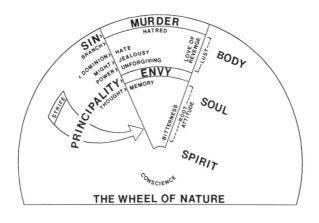

THE WHEEL OF NATURE

Chapter 18

THE END OF REBELLION

*But the fearful, and unbelieving, and abominable, and murderers, and whoremongers, and **sorcerers**, and idolaters, and all liars, shall have their part in the lake which burneth with fire and brimstone…* (Revelation 21:8).

We now come to the last sin category, sorcery. Samuel helps us understand this sin in his rebuke of Saul:

Behold, to obey is better than sacrifice, and to hearken than the fat of rams. For rebellion is as the sin of witchcraft… (1 Samuel 15:22-23).

The seriousness, and also the end, or result, of rebellion is seen in God's command to Israel concerning their rebellious sons:

*If a man have a stubborn and rebellious son, which will not obey the voice of his father, or the voice of his mother, and that, when they have chastened him, will not hearken unto them: Then shall his father and his mother lay hold on him, and bring him out unto the elders of his city, and unto the gate of his place; And they shall say unto the elders of his city, This our son is **stubborn and rebellious**, he will not obey our voice; he is a **glutton**, and a **drunkard**. And all the men of his city shall stone him with stones, that he die: so shalt thou put evil away from* *among you; and all Israel shall hear, and fear* (Deuteronomy 21:18-21).

The dominion spirit discussed in the last chapter was hatred. Hatred causes a person to rebel against those he hates if they are in authority over him. Like all dominions, the evil spirit of hatred opens people's hearts to the influence of the next principality.

To understand how satan does this we need to review what we have already learned about hatred: *Hatred is murder!* The Bible equates hate and murder in 1 John 3:15: *"Whosoever hateth his brother is a murderer...."* Malachi 2:10 teaches that all humans are brothers. We cannot hate another person and be saved! We must forgive. This is not optional; it is required. Micah 6:8 says:

> *He hath showed thee, O man, what is good; and what doth the Lord **require** of thee, but to do justly, and to love **mercy**, and to walk **humbly** with thy God?*

People cannot do as Cain and simply rise up and kill their brothers without being punished (see 1 John 3:11-12). Therefore, when people harbor roots of bitterness in their hearts, but they know they cannot get away with murder, they will attempt to destroy those whom they hate some other way. One way they accomplish this is by dominating and controlling them. People who are completely controlled by someone else do not have a life of their own. In other words, their lives are taken from them through the other person's control.

An animal is normally eaten after it is killed, becoming part of the body of the person who consumes it. Likewise, the object of sorcery is to consume its victims and make them a part of the person who obtains dominion over them.

When Jeremiah spoke the judgmental Word of God to his sinful brethren, they were offended at him. Instead of repenting, they hated him and decided to destroy his prophetic voice:

> *Then said they, "Come, and let us devise devices against Jeremiah; for the law shall not perish from the priest, nor counsel*

from the wise, nor the word from the prophet. Come, and let us smite him with the tongue, and let us not give heed to any of his words" (Jeremiah 18:18).

The mistaken attitude that it is better to be *independent* of authority and its representative than to be in submission leads to rebellion. This can be seen in the above Scripture. They resented the Law, the counsel of the wise, and the Word of God. They also hated God's spokesman, the prophet.

Stubborn self-will (not giving heed to any of God's Words) is revealed in this Scripture. Something far more aggressive is also revealed. Those rebellious men devised evil devices against Jeremiah and smote him with their words. Stubbornly refusing to obey is *passive* resistance—rebellion is *active* resistance. To successfully rebel against authority and be independent, people must gain control over those they are supposed to obey.

When people gain control and rule over those whom they should submit to, they commit sin. *Selfish exercise of authority that belongs to others is sorcery.* Yet, to be independent, people must control others instead of being controlled.

If people are not in authority, they are automatically under authority and, therefore, not independent. To successfully be independent, people have to be in control. The attitude that independence is good and that it should be pursued is the motivating "leg" of the scorpion within people.

The lust for dominion (to be in charge of others and, therefore, in control of one's own life) is the "eye" of the evil scorpion of humanity's nature. This inherent desire drives people to rebel. Passive resistance is not enough.

When people want to be at the helm of their own ship, they must mutiny against the legitimate Captain. All people are under authority, and all proper authority is of God (see Rom. 13:1-2). All people have a Captain, and often, many captains (see 1 Cor. 11:3).

To fully understand rebellion (which is the branch of sorcery), we must first have a proper understanding of authority. The Scriptures command everyone to be obedient to the higher powers, or authorities. Every human being is under God's authority as expressed in His Word and by His Spirit. *The head of every person is Christ (saved or lost)*. Also, all people are responsible to obey their own consciences (see Acts 24:16). Next, civil government (federal, state, and local) must be obeyed. After that, husbands are over their wives, and parents are over their own children (see 1 Cor. 11:3; Eph. 5:22, 6:1-6).

There are many other rulers, or authorities, but in every case authority should be divided properly. Employers, pastors, school teachers, and many others have authority in certain areas of people's lives.

An example of rightly dividing authority is seen in comparing employers and pastors. *Employers* have no responsibility over the souls of their employees; therefore, they should not tell them where to go to church or how to worship.

Likewise, *pastors (elders)* cannot legitimately tell the people under them where to work. Also, because elders have no authority over their neighboring churches' flocks, they have no responsibility to lead, feed, or heal them. God holds them accountable only for those sheep who submit to the authority He has invested in them (see Heb. 13:17).

All authority is limited to the responsibility under it. For example, because pastors are not responsible to supply natural substance (food, clothing, and shelter) for those in their congregations who are able to work, they have no authority in those areas. To assume authority over any area of people's lives where there is no corresponding responsibility is to usurp authority in that area. Someone is responsible and therefore has authority. Authority without responsibility creates tyrants, or dictators.

On the other hand, people are guaranteed frustration if they are held responsible for something that they have no authority to control. A school teacher who is not allowed to discipline the children she is responsible to teach is a good example. People should have authority to oversee that for which they are responsible. But, if they simply *feel* responsible, but in reality are not, they will feel compelled to assume control. Wives are especially susceptible to this snare. If a woman's husband does not assume his proper place of natural authority in the home and bear his responsibilities as he should, often she will assume his place of control. Two wrongs do not make a right. If she assumes headship, she is out of her place, regardless of her circumstances.

Wives who assume responsibility for their husband's salvation is another example of this snare. They often fall into the trap of trying to *make* their husbands serve God. When God makes people responsible for something, He automatically gives them authority to do whatever is necessary to carry out their duties. Wives who are trying to be their husbands' *"Holy Spirit,"* dutifully trying to convict them into repentance, are in error.

Peter teaches wives the proper way to reach their loved ones. They are responsible *to be a witness* to their husbands. They are *not* to teach, preach, persuade, or exhort. To do these things is to assume authority that God has not given (see 1 Cor. 7:13-16):

> *Likewise, ye wives, be in subjection to your own husbands;*
> *that if any obey not the word, they also may without the word*
> *be won by the conversation* [lifestyle] *of the wives* (1 Peter
> 3:1).

A wife cannot be responsible (and therefore in authority) and be in submission at the same time. This is true whether she is concerned with her husband's salvation or with providing the natural, material goods for her family. God holds the husband accountable for the welfare of the family when he is able to provide for them, not the wife (see 1 Tim. 5:8).

When there is a conflict, wives who work for employers other than their husbands usually become confused as to who they are required to obey. The answer to this is simple: the husband has final authority over the natural aspects of his wife's life, and she is commanded to be obedient to him (see 1 Cor. 14:34; 1 Pet. 3:1).

Although a man's wife can operate under delegated authority, her husband is still held responsible for that which he has delegated to her. Likewise, women in ministry may serve in any capacity delegated to them as long as they are under the authority of the men God holds accountable for their service (see Rom. 16:1-6; 1 Tim. 2:12; Heb. 13:17; Rev. 2:20).

Principality (Rule)

When people, male or female, resist the authorities that are over the various aspects of their lives, they fall into the snare of the devil. The dominion of hatred opens their hearts to the influence of a spirit of **witchcraft**. This evil spirit persuades them that they should be the ones to decide their fate, not their parents, husband, employer, pastor, governor, or anyone else.

To be the one at the helm, they must gain control. *In order to be in control, people devise devices to aid themselves in gaining control* (see Jer. 18:18). These devices can be one of a number of different mechanisms. The Bible reveals several.

*Probably the most common device used is **fear**.* Fear can be induced through threats, blows, loud words, or even sullen silence. Fear casts a spell over people and brings them into bondage. Having bound them, their conquerors can then make them do whatever they desire.

Using force and power, anger, or any aggressive device that invokes fear into another for the sake of gaining illegitimate control over them is witchcraft (see Ezra 4:18-23; Neh. 6:7-13). Proverbs 29:25 warns, *"The fear of man bringeth a snare...."* It does not matter if this apprehension is the fear of rejection, the fear of the loss of the honor of people, or the fear of people's anger; all three bring people into bondage and under the spell of witchcraft.

Satan even uses religion, or the fear of hell, to cast his insidious spell upon people. Paul referred to this tactic of satan in his letter to the Galatians: *"O foolish Galatians, who hath bewitched you, that ye should not obey the truth..."* (Gal. 3:1; see also Gal. 2:4).

184

Bewitching **charm** *is also a witchcraft device that is quite common.* Although both males and females are subject to using this spell, it is used by females more often than males. Both sexes are subject to a spirit of witchcraft's charm, but men are more likely to fall victims to its enchantments (see Judg. 16:5,15-17). Proverbs 7:10-21 gives us an example of this evil device of satan:

> *With her much fair speech she caused him to yield, with the flattering of her lips **she forced him** (Proverbs 7:21).*

Another deceitful device that a spirit of witchcraft may use is **hypochondria.** Pretending to be sick or weak, hypochondriacs invoke the emotion of pity in those whom they desire to overcome. Amnon used this ploy to entice his half-sister into his room before he raped her. He pretended that he was sick to bring her under his evil spell (see 2 Sam. 13:3-15).

A husband or wife using fake headaches to avoid rendering *"due benevolence"* to his or her spouse is another example of this witchcraft device. The wife does not have authority over her own body, and likewise, the husband's body is his wife's, according to the covenant agreement of marriage (see 1 Cor. 7:2-5).

Guilt, *too, can be used to control others.* This powerful device is especially effective in controlling relatives. An abusive husband tries to make his wife feel that all of their problems are *"all her fault."* Wives and mothers also use guilt to control. Children are often easy victims of selfish parents who use this wicked tool.

Tears *are another common witchcraft device.* Tears are frequently used by women to control their husbands, employers, or other male companions (see Judg. 14:17). This device is formed early in life. Children often attempt to manipulate their parents with tears.

Bargaining, *or* **bribery**, *is another means of gaining control.* Simon the sorcerer tried to bribe Peter, attempting to regain the control of the people of Samaria (see Acts 8:9-11,18-23). Money is a very powerful tool that the god of this world uses in his efforts to control people (see 1 Sam. 12:3).

Some people jokingly refer to this world's *"golden rule"*—*"He that has the gold makes the rule":*

> *For wisdom is a defense, and money is a defense: but the excellency of knowledge is, that wisdom giveth life to them that have it* (Ecclesiastes 7:12).

Two other very evil devices of witchcraft that need to be guarded against are **alcohol** *and* **drugs**. These substances have cast their spell over many pitiful souls, including the very ones who have the witchcraft spirits. Once people come under the influence and power of these substances, they become addicted (a servant to satan) through them (see Prov. 20:1, 23:29-35; Isa. 28:7).

Power (Authority)

Once people have fallen prey to the influence (spell) of a spirit of witchcraft, their hearts are open to the deceptive spirit of *infirmity*. This spirit exercises control over his victims' members and utilizes the weakness of their flesh to keep them under his authority.

To properly understand this spirit, remember that infirmity means more than just sickness. It actually means feebleness, or weakness. Although sickness is indeed an infirmity, there are many weaknesses of the flesh's nature that are not sicknesses. Jesus said, *"...The spirit indeed is willing, but the flesh is weak"* (Matt. 26:41). Paul referred to this weakness in Romans 6:19:

> *I speak after the manner of men because of the infirmity* [weakness] *of your flesh: for as ye have yielded your members servants to uncleanness and to iniquity unto iniquity; even so now yield your members servants to righteousness unto holiness* (Romans 6:19).

Because sickness is sometimes a product of a spirit of infirmity, to fully understand this spirit, a discussion of sickness as recorded in the Bible is necessary. For example, deafness was first in the spirit, then in the body as a disease. Blindness is another infirmity that was first introduced into the world in spirit form. Then it was manifested in the natural eyes of people (see Lev. 26:15-16; Lam. 5:17). Likewise, many other sicknesses and physical infirmities are the results of humanity's rebellion against God's authority and rule (see Exod. 15:26; Num. 12:1-15; 2 Chron. 16:10-12, 21:12-19, 26:16-21).

Often the spirit of infirmity works in and through the vertebrae to disrupt the victim's health. Back pains and many sicknesses that result from pinched nerves in the backbone are sometimes (but not always) the work of a spirit of infirmity (see Luke 13:11-13,16).

When people yield to satan's spell and *bow their backs* against the authorities over them, they yield their backs to a spirit of infirmity (see Rom. 11:9-10). *This is not to imply that all back trouble is induced by demons or caused by sin.* There are many different causes of sicknesses—some are named in the Bible—some are not. Blindness, deafness, foot trouble, stomach problems, and many more diseases and sicknesses are recorded in Scripture. Many were caused by sin. Some were not (see 2 Kings 13:14; 1 Tim. 5:23).

For instance, Isaac was blind in his old age (see Gen. 27:1). The Scriptures do not say that he sinned or that he had a demon. But many of the sicknesses Jesus healed were caused by demons. As all other subjects taught in the Word of God—this, too, should be rightly and carefully divided (see Matt. 12:22; John 9:1-3; Acts 10:38; 2 Tim. 2:15).

Another very common manifestation of the spirit of infirmity is impatience. This weakness of the flesh is revealed in people's unwillingness to wait for those things that appease their fleshly appetites. Impatience opens people's hearts to provocation by the next evil spirit more than any other attribute of the flesh's nature (see Ps. 37:7; Luke 21:19; Heb. 10:36, 12:1).

Might

Once people are under the authority of the spirit of infirmity, they are subject to the powerful spirit of **anger**, which works through their *emotions* to control them (see Eccl. 7:9). This demon's spell also works upon and through people to make others obey them through fear.

Although some people have thought they were just *"hot-tempered,"* the Word of God teaches that all people are of like passion (see James 5:17). Redheaded and Irish people are not subject to anger any more than bald-headed or English people are. The devil uses such myths to hide his involvement in the lives of those he has deceived.

When people yield their rights to those under them or rightly yield to the authorities over them, the demon of anger is disarmed. When he is disarmed through people's obedience to godly principles, he cannot overcome them through their *"temper."*

One of the ways a spirit of anger expresses himself is with profanity. This spirit motivates people to curse when they are not *"having things their own way."* The evil backlash of this sin is revealed in Psalm 109:17-19:

> *As he loved cursing, so let it come unto him…As he clothed himself with cursing like as with his garment, so let it come into his bowels like water, and like oil into his bones. Let it be unto him as the garment which covers him…continually* (Psalm 109:17-19).

The spirit of anger not only expresses himself through cursing, but also hurls threats and accusations and sometimes even blows upon those his wrath is directed toward. Sullen, silent withdrawal is another manifestation of this evil spirit. Some people do not speak to the people they are angry with for days or even years!

Besides provoking people to slam doors, curse people and machines, raise their voices at those they love, and sulk, this demon also causes them to murmur. Murmuring is witchcraft prayer. Like cursing, it destroys people's blessings (see Isa. 8:19-22).

Although some people would not curse under any circumstances, they still give place to the spirit of anger by murmuring and complaining.

Grumbling is evil. This spirit repeatedly robbed Israel in the wilderness (see Exod. 15:24, 16:2, 17:3; Deut. 1:27, 28:47-48).

Dominion (Mastery)

Finally, when people rebel and succumb to the desire for control, they come under the dominion *spirit* of **control**. This spirit develops various manipulative ways of thinking so that people can, *"have their own way"*— but to their own hurt—at their own expense!

> *If ye be willing and obedient, ye shall eat the good of the land:*
> *But if ye refuse and rebel, ye shall be devoured with the sword:*
> *for the mouth of the Lord hath spoken it* (Isaiah 1:19-20).

The various manifestations of a controlling spirit are almost too numerous to mention, but it is important to recognize that people with a controlling spirit will consistently interfere in the lives of others. Often this is done in such subtle and persuasive ways that the people being harmed are not even aware of the control. Likewise, the people interfering frequently do not realize that they are causing harm (that is, in their own, conscious mind). Their consciences are seared through self-justification so that they will not heed the feelings of shame or guilt that the conscience tries to correct them with.

Here are a few, common manifestations of controlling spirits. People with this spirit promptly take control of events, even though they have no authority to do so; frequently tell others how to do things without being asked for advice; habitually borrow without asking permission (and often do not return whatever they have borrowed); take and use others' property as though it is their own (and often without so much as a *"thank you"*); have to have their way in just about every situation. All of these are common manifestations of this spirit's presence. The people with the spirit seldom know that they have the spirit working within their personality.

There are two specific examples of sorcery found in the book of Acts— Simon Margas and Barjesus (see Acts 8:9-11,18, 13:6-8). We also have two modern examples that are much more recent—Jim Jones and David Koresh. Hopefully, no one reading this will ever be faced with such deception and its tragic results like their followers were, but, be careful! There are many other deceivers today, though less obvious, who nonetheless, are still ruling others for their own gain.

Although we are studying the last segment of the Wheel of Nature (sorcery), we should note that, like all other dominion spirits, the spirit of control opens people's hearts to the influence of the principality which follows him. This principality is the spirit of error, the instigator of idolatry.

Satan used Eve's desire for intimate knowledge to gain control of Adam's authority over the world. The spirit of control causes people to desire position, wealth, and knowledge to gain power. Through the power of such things as money and knowledge, people attempt to gain independence. Their mistaken attitude is that independence is good. Their mistaken belief is that things like money and knowledge will bring independence (see 1 Cor. 12:25-27).

It is this aspect of sorcery that explains why idolatry is invariably associated with witchcraft. *"...Covetousness...is idolatry"* (Col. 3:5). This truth also gives us an understanding of how the spirit of anger (which works under witchcraft) was working in the very first category of sin, idolatry. (Laban was angry over the theft of his images, or household gods.)

The motion of the Wheel of Nature is perpetual. Regardless of where or in what manner it starts, it will always continue its rotation. Jesus said that whenever anyone overcomes one of sin's strongmen, the demon returns with seven of his fellows. Their combined wickedness far exceeds the first spirit's mischief (see Luke 11:24-26).

People cannot ignore sin. Regardless of what area of the flesh's nature it dwells in, sin will always increase unto more ungodliness. God said that if any one of the original inhabitants are left in the land, they will rise up and become strong. By taking back all they have lost, they bring people back into slavery to do their evil will. People cannot compromise with sin.

"Whosoever commits sin is the servant of sin" (see Num. 33:55; Josh. 23:5-13; Prov. 14:9; John 8:34).

The Witch-Wimp Syndrome

No study of sorcery would be complete without an introduction of Queen Jezebel and King Ahab. The witch-wimp syndrome is defined by them. Almost everyone has heard (or known) of a *"Jezebel* and *Ahab."*

Jezebel was the daughter of a foreign king. She apparently married Ahab for the purpose of controlling Israel through his throne. Wimp Ahab allowed her to rule and ruin Israel through the authority of his office. The legacy of this infamous couple is summed up in 1 Kings 21:25-26:

> *But there was none like unto Ahab, which did sell himself to work wickedness in the sight of the Lord, **whom Jezebel his wife stirred up**. And he did very abominably in following idols, according to all things as did the Amorites, whom the Lord cast out before the children of Israel* (1 Kings 21:25-26).

Jezebel's *anger* is well documented. Even Elijah fled from before her wrath after his famous victory on Mount Carmel. It was Jezebel who threatened his life after he killed the evil prophets of Baal (see 1 Kings 19:1-3). The book of Revelation reveals even more about this woman's wickedness. She taught the people of Israel to commit idolatry and fornication (see Rev. 2:20).

Satan used a Queen (Jezebel) in a King's office (Ahab's) to bring God's people into idolatry and fornication. When Ahab submitted to Jezebel, he sinned. Likewise, satan used a person (Eve), in a position God did not place her in, to overthrow the first works of God. When Adam gave place to his wife and did not bear rule in his home, he sinned (see Gen. 3:17; also see Esther 1:15-22).

When wives usurp and use the authority that God has delegated to their husbands, they commit sorcery. When employees, through the force and power of collective agreement, control employers, they sin. When anyone controls the person or people whom God has placed them under, they commit sorcery. *"There is no power* [authority] *but of God: the powers that be are ordained of God"* (Rom. 13:1). To rebel against God (God-given authority) is sorcery.

It is even a sin to speak evil of those who are in authority! To despise government and to speak evil of dignities is iniquity. People cannot murmur against Moses without sinning (see Exod. 16:8; Acts 23:5; 2 Pet. 2:10). Likewise, the office of president, governor, etc. must be honored.

We should be aware that usurping authority is not limited to subordinates. A pastor or other minister who dominates, ruling without being in submission to fellow elders, is also in error. Spiritual rulers are *not* to be lords over God's sheep (see Acts 15:6,22-23; 1 Tim. 5:17; 1 Pet. 5:2-3):

> *But Jesus called them unto Him, and said, "Ye know that the princes of the Gentiles exercise dominion over them, and they that are great exercise authority upon them. But it shall not be so among you: but whosoever will be great among you, let him be your minister; and whosoever will be chief among you, let him be your servant"* (Matthew 20:25-27).

Notice that Jesus said *"let"* him be your minister. All submission is to be voluntary. People are to *"let"* themselves be ministered to. Jesus, as well as Peter and Paul, gave Christians the right instructions so that sorcery will not be a factor in their church government—that is, if they establish their government according to God's Word.

Because all legitimate authority is of God and God is love, the proper exercise of authority will always bless those who are subject to that authority. Husbands are required to rule their homes in love. Marriage does not give husbands a license to be dictators. They are responsible to consider their wives' counsel. Employers are also held accountable for the way they exercise authority over those who work for them (see Rom. 13:1; Eph. 5:25, 6:4,9). Sorcery is not limited to a few Jezebels.

Sin—Sorcery

Lust (Eye)—Love of Dominion

Root (Leg)—Love of Independence

Branch (Motion)—Rebellion

Spirits

Principality (Rule)—Witchcraft

Power (Authority)—Infirmity

Might (Miracle Power)—Anger

Dominion (Mastery)—Control

Fruits

Murmuring; Complaining; Profanity; Cunning manipulation; Charm; Flattery; Tears; Bargaining

Some Common Sins in this Category

Drunkenness; Drug addiction; Bribery; Vandalism; Violence; Cursing; Hypochondria; Speaking against rulers

THE WHEEL OF NATURE

Chapter 19

AN OPEN DOOR

No other biblical character uncovers and reveals the process of iniquity, and God's judgment for sin, more clearly than King David. What would cause a man who had everything—wealth, honor, fame, and power—to turn to forbidden fruit? David was a man after God's own heart. He loved and served God; yet, like so many others that God anointed to rule, he fell for a woman. What led to his fall?

Adam, God's first son, fell through his relationship with his wife. *Samson*, God's strongest deliverer, blundered through his weakness for Delilah (*Delilah* means feeble). *Solomon*, God's wisest king, was deceived by his wives. And *David*, a man after God's own heart, allowed satan to fill his heart with lust. David sinned in every category of iniquity, becoming ensnared by idolizing a woman named Bathsheba.

By examining David's impulsive fall into sin, we can observe the entire process of iniquity in operation. As we began, remember that rejection opens a person's heart to a low self-image. This activates the natural desire to conquer. Striving to *"prove"* themselves provokes people to try to excel above their peers. They may try to gain superiority through such means as athletic or political victories, catching trophy fish, or even, as in David's case, sleeping with someone else's spouse!

Both rejection and the compulsion to conquer are evident in David's upbringing. When God sent Samuel to select a king for Israel, He sent him to the house of Jesse, David's father. But David was not there. He was in the field on that all important day when Samuel came to appoint and anoint Israel's second king. His father did not esteem David worthy to even be there for the selection (see 1 Sam. 16:5,11).

David was also left at home when his brothers went to war. He was accounted only as an errand boy to supply their needs. Later, David was scorned by his brothers for just appearing on the battlefield (see 1 Sam. 17:17-18;28-32).

Being rejected, David was ambitious to excel among his peers. It is no wonder that he was quick to accept Goliath's challenge. This is not to say that David was any less of a man of faith or courage. God makes all of His children's circumstances work together for their good (see Gen. 50:20; Rom. 8:28).

Even after David defeated Goliath, his self-esteem was still low and his self-image still marred by past rejection. This is evident in his reply to King Saul when Saul asked him to marry his daughter:

> *Who am I? And what is my life, or my father's family in Israel,*
> *that I should be son in law to the King?* (1 Samuel 18:18)

David also suffered rejection from King Hanun. This is recorded immediately before the account of his fall into sin. Still smarting from Hanun's rejection, David was easy prey for satan's snare (see 2 Sam 10:1-4). His only defense would have been to forgive King Hanun. To harbor bitterness in the heart always leads to defilement (see Eccl. 7:26; Heb. 12:13-16).

God's Word paints a very clear picture as it records the setting for what King David thought would be a secret affair:

> *And it came to pass...when kings go forth to battle* [to con-
> quer]*...that David arose from off his bed and walked upon*
> *the roof of the king's house: and from the roof he saw a woman*
> *washing herself; and the woman was very beautiful to look*
> *upon* (2 Samuel 11:1-2).

David was conditioned to be a conqueror by the circumstances he suffered. He was formed through rejection to be an ambitious servant of God. God's intent was for David to conquer Israel's enemies. But, instead, satan worked to refocus David's desire, directing it toward his neighbor's wife. In this way, satan brought down another of God's faithful (see Prov. 7:25-27).

David *idolized* Bathsheba when he saw her bathing in the courtyard and was enticed into *adultery* by his lust. When she became pregnant, he *feared* he would lose the *honor* of his subjects because of his lowly deed and tried to cover his sin. He justified himself instead of repenting.

David's conscience condemned him; therefore, he tried to hide his sin by calling Uriah home from war. After all attempts to *deceive* Uriah into thinking the child Bathsheba carried was his, David betrayed his loyal servant unto death. He *murdered* him with the sword of his enemies. Then, *taking dominion* over his fallen soldier's household, he married Bathsheba and added her to his harem (see 2 Sam. 11:1-27).

God's reproof of David further unveils his sin of scornful self-righteousness. God, identifying with Uriah, twice accused David of *despising* Him:

> *Wherefore hast thou despised the commandment of the Lord, to do evil in his sight? Thou hast killed Uriah the Hittite with the sword, and hast taken his wife to be thy wife, and hast slain him with the sword of the children of Ammon. Now therefore the sword shall never depart from thine house; because thou hast despised me, and hast taken the wife of Uriah the Hittite to be thy wife* (2 Samuel 12:9-10).

Because David refused and defied the counsel of his conscience, he continued to sin even after being convicted in his heart. Through his stubborn self-will and the fear of losing the honor of his peers, he hardened his heart and repeated the sins of King Saul, who had ruled before him—rebellion and stubborn unbelief.

Remember, people accuse others of the same sin that is in their own hearts. *Then they are put in the state of the judgments they make.* When David was young he was one of Saul's servants. Even though he was a faithful servant, Saul tried to kill him. David judged Saul for this. Then he fell into the snare of his own judgment and did that which he judged Saul for—he killed his own loyal servant: faithful, innocent Uriah (see 1 Sam. 18:11, 24:11-12; 2 Sam. 11:22-25).

When David was confronted by Nathan with a parable depicting his sin, he quickly became angry at the traveler's host in the parable. Upon seeing himself and his own sin mirrored in the heart of the selfish rich man in Nathan's story, he judged himself worthy of death. He pronounced his own death sentence and fined himself to fully repay, in this world, for the injustice done to his fellow man (see Matt. 12:37; 2 Sam. 12:1-14).

Then God spoke: *"Thou art the man"* (2 Sam. 12:7). David's heart was smitten with guilt, and he instantly repented. But God's gift of life, freely and instantly given upon David's repentance and confession, did not take away the bitter fruit of his sin. God said that the sword would never depart from his house. David paid for his error, indeed, in the final analysis, he paid double for his sin (see Prov. 17:13, Isa. 40:2). He lost his wives and his sons, and his reputation was marred forever (see Prov. 6:32-33).

There is a common misconception in the Church today that repentance annuls God's promise of reaping what one sows. This too is a deception of satan. Once people sin they are under the curse of eternal damnation through the *Universal Law of Death, "The soul that sinneth, it shall die..."* (Ezek. 18:20; see also Gen. 2:17). God, however, in His abundant mercies, has paid the death penalty for people through the cross of Christ.

Likewise, there is no more curse if people have repented, confessed their sins, and forgiven those who have wronged them. Jesus removed the punishment of the Law, *but He did not remove the bitter fruit, or results, of sin.*

The fruit of the tree of sin is the product of what people have sown, *both naturally and spiritually.* For instance, an alcoholic's family is not instantly healed of the trauma they suffered just because the drinking parent repents. The tree of sin dies when the roots are severed, but the bitter fruit remains and it must be dealt with. In like manner, a prisoner is not instantly pardoned just because he repents. He must still pay his debt to society.

The gift of God is eternal life, and the sting of the scorpion is eternal damnation—death in the final sense of the word (see Rom. 6:23; 1 Cor. 15:55-56; James 1:15). The cross of Christ abolished the death penalty and the curse of punishment for all who come unto God by Jesus, but this did not change the *Universal Law of Harvest* (see Gen. 8:22; Ps. 103:10-12; 2 Tim. 1:10):

> *Be not deceived; God is not mocked: for whatsoever a man soweth, that shall he also reap. For he that soweth to his flesh shall of the flesh reap corruption; but he that soweth to the Spirit shall of the Spirit reap life everlasting* (Galatians 6:7-8).

Like all 12 of the Universal Laws of the Universe, this Law cannot be broken. It can only be illustrated.

David was King of Israel; therefore, when David sinned satan received authority to promote sin in the nation. Satan, without delay, began to work iniquity in Israel through his newly acquired license. Through the Law of Dominion, the wicked one now had an open door to all of God's sheep that were under David's rule. His evil influence was immediately evident in Jerusalem.

Satan cannot work until someone lets him in. Once he is allowed in, he must be thrown out. David quickly repented, and satan's recently acquired authority was instantly severed. However, satan had already slipped in through the door. David still had to reap the fruit of his sin.

The King's wickedness was now apparent in his sons. David's example of deceitfulness did not go unnoticed in his home—hypocrisy fools only the hypocrite. David's authorization of sin into the kingdom began working evil in his own household.

David's son Amnon deceived and raped his half sister, Tamar. Amnon's brother Absalom, David's favorite son, killed Amnon, but the evil did not stop then. Absalom, lusting for power and ambitious for the honor of people, began to work deceitfully. He did as his father had done, only this time the plot was against David. Enticing the people of the kingdom to follow him, Absalom raised insurrection against his father. But, he failed in his purposes, and after taking David's wives, he was killed. David lost two for one. He lost two sons for Uriah, and his daughter and wives were defiled because he disgraced the wife of his servant, Uriah.

Through Christ, repentance gives life—complete pardon from the death penalty. Nevertheless, the Word of God declares that people must still eat the fruit of their own thoughts, words, and deeds (see Prov. 18:20-21; Isa. 3:10; Jer. 6:19, 17:10).

Jesus died because the Law of Death cannot be broken—sin always brings forth death. Jesus paid the debt that we could not pay. Nevertheless, all people must reap the fruit of their own sins in this life. The Universal Law of Harvest cannot be broken. Instead, it is illustrated each time one of God's commandments is disobeyed.

In the conquest of Canaan, Judah captured King Adonibezek and cut off his thumbs and big toes. Adonibezek commented:

> *Threescore and ten kings, having their thumbs and their great toes cut off, gathered their meat under my table: as I have done, so God hath requited me... (Judges 1:7).*

The cross of Christ does not release people from the Law of Harvest. Although one of the thieves on the cross beside Jesus repented, he was still crucified. He was not taken down. He was pardoned through repentance and justified by faith; therefore, he received eternal life, but he still ate the bitter fruit of his sin. In his case, the fruit was an early death.

Perhaps the repentant thief himself, while rebuking his partner in crime, expressed this unchanging Law best:

*Dost not thou fear God, seeing thou art in the same condemnation? **And we indeed justly; for we receive the due reward of our deeds...** (Luke 23:40-41).*

Paul persecuted the Church unmercifully. He imprisoned the saints, beat them, stoned them, and made them blaspheme—then payday came. Paul reaped persecution continually. He spent much of his life in prison. His persecutors scourged him beyond his ability to keep count of the stripes. They even stoned him and left him for dead. He, too, reaped what he sowed—everyone does (see Acts 26:9-11; 2 Cor. 11:23-25).

Jacob is another good example of the working of this eternal Law. Jacob deceived his father and in the process cheated his father's favorite son, Esau, out of a blessing. Also, for a pot of food, Jacob persuaded Esau to sell him the inheritance his brother was to receive. Esau later repented with bitter tears, but was denied the inheritance which he sold through his folly (see Gen. 25:31-33, 27:18-24;35-36; Heb. 12:16-17).

But in due process of time, the seeds of deception that Jacob had sown brought forth their evil harvest. Jacob's sons deceived him and sold his own favorite son, Joseph, into slavery. Through envy, they hardened their hearts against their brother's cries. Jacob, having lost his beloved son, wept bitter tears. Then because of a famine, he had to leave his ill-gotten portion of the inheritance to get food. Jacob, an old, bitter man, died in the land of Egypt (see Gen. 37:3,27-35, 47:8-9; Acts 7:9).

The deceitful sons of Jacob and their children became slaves in the very nation into which they sold their brother. Then their descendants paid back the money Jacob's sons had coveted and received for their brother's anguish, with usury. They had to build Pharaoh treasure cities for recompense (see Gen. 47:18-27; Exod. 1:9-11).

Many years later, Jacob's descendants groaned under the heavy load of the fruit of their forefathers' sins. When they had completely paid their ancestors' debt, God, moved with compassion, released them. By giving them the ordinance of Passover, He showed them the way to freedom. But it was not until they killed the Passover lamb, shed his blood, and applied it upon their door posts that they were freed from the bondage inherited through their forefathers' sins (see Exod. 12:5-11).

Many of God's people are still planting evil seed. Sinning in secret, they do not understand that the Laws of the Universe are absolute—they cannot be broken. God's commandments were given to keep people from breaking themselves upon these Laws (see Num. 32:23).

God's commandments can be broken. When people do break them, they illustrate to themselves and to the world that God's eternal, Universal Laws are infallible (see Ps. 119:89).

The Process of Iniquity

Although we have examined the process of sin step by step, like dissecting a frog in a laboratory, the actual works, or motions, of sin are much more complex (see Rom. 7:5; Gal. 5:19-21). We examined each attribute of the flesh, with its attending spirit, in progressive order (see 1 Kings 20:1,23-25). In the actual working of iniquity, several demon spirits from different categories often work together instead of one always following the other.

A close examination of the motions of sin reveals simultaneous activity among demons. Several principalities, along with their subordinate spirits, work together at the same time to accomplish their evil when they can (see Gen. 3:1-5). But, the same pattern which is established in each individual sin is found in the overall work of satan.

This pattern is first reason, then imagination, followed by emotion, and then memory. The principalities of *error* and *lying* work together through *reasoning* to tempt people to sin. By displacing and replacing the righteous counsel of the human spirit, they give people seemingly logical reasons why they are right and the conscience is wrong (see Gen. 3:4-5). When people hold the truth in their hearts and refuse the error of these two demons, they usually will not sin. But once they are deceived by one or both of them, the actual process of iniquity begins its evil, relentless process.

After they succumb to the influence of these first two principalities and come under the authority of their subordinates, the principalities of *slumber* and *haughtiness* are able to work through their *imaginations* to bring them deeper into iniquity. These two spirits, working through the desires of the flesh, cause people to sin against themselves and others. In their ignorance of God's Universal Laws, people foolishly despise their fellows as they trespass against them (see Matt. 12:36-37; 1 Cor. 6:18; Eph. 2:3).

The principalities of *fear* and *envy* then work through people's *emotions* to motivate them to seek their own safety and gain, with little concern for their neighbors' feelings. Working through the desires and ambitions of people's carnal minds, these demons propel them onward toward the fullness of iniquity.

Then the principalities of *perverseness* and *witchcraft* work through their *memories* to train and enslave them. These spirits develop habitual patterns of thinking, producing specific reactions in their victims' lives. These conditioned responses addict them and cause them to continue in sin.

The first pair of principalities, error and lying, work by displacing and replacing the counsel of the human *spirit*. The second pair, slumber and haughtiness, work through the passions of the *flesh*. The third pair, fear and envy, work through the ambitions of the *carnal mind*. The last two, perversion and witchcraft, work their evil through the *soul* by developing conditioned responses within the mind.

Paul said that a Christian's warfare was with principalities and powers (see Eph. 6:12). We can see that if the first two principalities of the spirit (error and lying) and the first two of the flesh (slumber and haughtiness) are overcome, satan's pattern is disrupted, and his demons are defeated. Thus we can see the wisdom of Paul's admonition:

> *(For the weapons of our warfare are not carnal, but mighty through God to the pulling down of strong holds;) casting down imaginations* [and logical reasoning], *and every high*

thing that exalteth itself against the knowledge of God, and
bringing into captivity every thought to the obedience of Christ
(2 Corinthians 10:4-5).

People's emotions are subject to reason and imagination. Because of this, if they cast down logical reasoning and vain imaginations that exalt themselves against the knowledge of God, the principalities of fear, perverseness, envy, and witchcraft have a difficult time convincing them to yield (see Rom. 1:21).

The Strongholds of Satan

Most strongholds result from demons from more than one category working together to produce a specific act of sin (see 2 Cor. 10:3-4). Various combinations of principalities work together with their subordinates to produce such bazaar behavior in humans as bulimia, compulsive gambling, and alcoholism.

We have already seen how the spirits of rejection and whoredoms work together to produce promiscuity and homosexuality. Another example previously discussed is rape. This sin is motivated by the spirits of whoredoms and hatred. Sadism (obtaining sexual pleasure from dominating, mistreating, or hurting one's partner) frequently results when a dominating spirit of control accompanies this pair. Sometimes psychological torture is used instead of physical pain.

Other combinations are gluttony and (self) hatred, which produce such abnormalities as bulimia. Suicidal thoughts are usually caused by (self) hatred and grief (although the hatred is usually directed toward someone else, such as a parent or spouse). Whoredoms and exhibitionism cause their victims to make obscene phone calls or to expose themselves indecently in public. Gluttony and the spirit of control, often working jointly with such spirits as grief, or jealously and hatred, can produce alcoholics (see Deut. 21:20; Prov. 20:1, 31:6-7; Luke 21:34).

Another less obvious stronghold example is Judas' sin, which was motivated by the greed of antichrist along with the passion of envy. These two treacherous spirits caused him to betray Jesus (see Matt. 27:18; John 12:4-6, 13:2).

Children are born with pure spirits. Satan, through his combined demon forces, uses a repetitious pattern in his attempts to take possession of their souls, or "land," so that he can make them servants of sin (see John 8:34; 2 Cor. 2:11).

Once people are captured and imprisoned by sin, the price of freedom is death. Jesus paid the demands of the Law of Death and bought back all who are willing to submit to His Lordship. When people are bought (saved) and delivered from sin through their covenant with God, God owns their "land." People's spirits are liberated in the process of salvation (see John 8:31-36; 1 Cor. 6:20).

Although we receive our freedom through the *Perfect Law of Liberty,* we must "take our liberty" from the inhabitants who have taken up residence in our land (see James 1:25). This process of deliverance is the violence that Jesus said existed in the Kingdom of God. He said, *"The kingdom of God is within you"* (Luke 17:21). As a result, spiritual warfare is also within us (see Matt. 11:12; Luke 4:18, 17:20-21; Gal. 5:17).

We can see this concept illustrated in the conquest of Canaan. God gave this land and its inhabitants to Israel. They had full ownership, but they did not have possession of the land until they took it by force. Once they drove out the inhabitants and occupied the land, they settled down to live in peace. But to maintain their peaceful existence, they had to be vigilant to keep it free from insurrection from within and invasion from without.

When Israel became careless and fell into sin, the original inhabitants grew strong and took back all they had lost. In addition, they enslaved the people of God, making them serve under their yoke. Those who were ordained to be the head soon became the tail (see Deut. 28:13-15,43-44; Judg. 2:1-15). Then God had to raise up judges to set them free. God, who never changes, is still working this same process of deliverance to liberate His people, today. The Church should pray for deliverers (see Judg. 2:16, 3:15, 4:3-7).

The Process of Iniquity

1. Temptation

   The five senses; (demonic) dreams; reason; imagination; emotion; memory

2. Deception—demons enter, producing the motions of sin

   a. Idolatry

   b. Fornication

   c. Fearful

3. Reason

   d. Unbelieving

4. Lies

   e. Lying

5. Self-Justification

   f. Abominable (Despising)

6. Accusation—to make a judgment

   g. Murder

7. Destruction—to be put in that state (judged)

   h. Sorcery

Chapter 20

THE PROCESS OF HEALING

For people to fully overcome the sinful nature, they must be healed of the results of the fall. God's children are promised healing in Second Chronicles 7:14, under certain conditions:

> *If My people, which are called by My name, shall humble them-*
> *selves, and pray, and seek My face, and turn from their wicked*
> *ways; then will I hear from heaven, and will forgive their sin,*
> *and will heal their land.*

Originally, all sickness—physical, emotional, and mental—came through sin (see Rom. 5:12-14). Overcoming our sin nature allows God's healing presence to work in our lives (see Ps. 103:2-3):

> *And they went out, and preached that men should repent. And*
> *they cast out many devils, and anointed with oil many that*
> *were sick, and healed them* (Mark 6:12-13).

> *And as ye go, preach, saying, "The kingdom of heaven is at*
> *hand." Heal the sick, cleanse the lepers, raise the dead, cast out*
> *devils: freely ye have received, freely give* (Matthew 10:7-8).

In this commandment, Jesus revealed a step-by-step process for total healing. *The first step is to submit to God and become a citizen of the Kingdom of Heaven.* When people do this, they have full covenant right to healing—spirit, soul, and body (see Exod. 15:25-26; Isa. 53:4-5).

Emotional Healing Consists Of:

1. Cleansing (Confession)

Cleansing is obtained through confession and forgiveness (see Ps. 103:31; John 1:9):

> *Having therefore these promises, dearly beloved, let us cleanse ourselves from all filthiness of the flesh and spirit, perfecting holiness in the fear of God* (2 Corinthians 7:1).

James brought confession and healing together by teaching the necessity of honest confession of people's trespasses before they could be healed:

> *Is any sick among you?...Confess your faults* [trespasses] *one to another, and pray one for another, that ye may be healed* (James 5:14,16).

The defilement of sin (see Tit. 1:15, Heb. 12:15), both guilt and bitterness, is cleansed by the blood of Jesus through faith (see Acts 15:9; Rom. 8:1; Heb. 9:14):

> *If we confess our sins, He is faithful and just to forgive us our sins, and to cleanse us from all unrighteousness* (1 John 1:9).

2. Restoration (Attitude Correction)

Restoration, or renewal, is raising that which is dead back to life (see Rom. 6:4). The spiritual minds people possessed as children must be renewed, or resurrected:

> *I beseech you therefore, brethren, by the mercies of God, that ye present your bodies a living sacrifice, holy, acceptable unto God, which is your reasonable service. And be not conformed to this world: but be ye transformed by the renewing of your mind...* (Romans 12:1-2).

Jesus said, *"I am the resurrection and the life"* (John 11:25). *I am*, not I have been or I will be! Jesus has given His followers life *now* and also the ability to restore life to those who were once alive but are now dead (see Rom. 5:17; 1 Pet. 4:10-11). This life is not only for the physical bodies of people—the dead and diseased are included—but people's souls and spirits are also subject to the quickening, present-tense power of God (see Rom. 8:11).

Consequently, Christ's servants can also raise anyone who is *dead in trespasses and sins* (see Eph. 2:1). Likewise, those dead and bound in the grave clothes of *tradition and religious formality* are also subject to the *"I am,"* ever-present, resurrection power of God (see 2 Cor. 1:19-20; Eph. 3:20, 5:14; Rev. 3:1).

3. Deliverance (Prayer)

Deliverance is casting out demons with the resulting peace this release brings (see Rom. 6:19; Col. 1:20-21):

> *For we wrestle not against flesh and blood, but against principalities, against powers, against the rulers of the darkness of this world, against spiritual wickedness in high places* (Ephesians 6:12).

For deliverance to be effective and lasting, it is essential to first bind a demon before casting it out (see Matt. 12:28-29). This is *not* done by saying a prayer like, *"In the name of Jesus, I bind you, satan"* or similar commands (see Acts 19:13-16). Whenever possible, the demon should be disarmed before exorcism (see Luke 11:22). He is disarmed by taking away his covenant rights (see Ps. 94:20; Prov. 26:2).

This is accomplished when those whom he has invaded confess their sins or their forefathers' sins (see Lev. 26:39-42; Prov. 28:13). Sin gave the demons the right to enter into their lives and, therefore, have authority over specific areas of their personalities (see Rom. 6:16; 2 Pet. 2:19).

Satan is disarmed through repentance, confession, and forgiveness. When this is completed, the cords of bondage causing people to be subject to impulsive or compulsive behaviors are broken and the demons are bound and led captive (see Prov. 5:22; Eph. 4:8). Then, through the prayer of agreement, the demons have to leave when they are commanded to do so (see Matt. 18:18-19; Luke 4:33-35). As a result, satan's covenant of sin is completely broken, and his demons have no right to return.

It should be obvious that for deliverance to be effective and the results lasting, counseling should precede the prayer of exorcism (see Luke 11:24-26; Mark 9:17,24-25). When this is not possible (in cases where the victims cannot participate in their own deliverance), counseling should follow the prayers (see Luke 8:35).

Those who claim that deliverance is "trying to cast out the flesh" should notice that Paul, when referring to this subject, specifically stated that we are *not* wrestling with flesh. *"For we wrestle not against flesh..."* (see Eph. 6:12). He taught that the cause of people's predicaments is spirits that work unrighteousness through their flesh (see Rom. 6:16,19; Eph. 6:11-12).

Others state, "A Christian cannot have a demon!" While we agree that Christians *should* not—the fact remains—many do. Second Corinthians 11:4 plainly states that Christians can receive other spirits even after they are saved and filled with the Holy Spirit. Demons live in and work through the flesh; God dwells in and works through the spirit (see Rom. 1:9; 1 Cor. 6:17).

Most Christians who have need of deliverance are *not* demon possessed; rather the Christians possess the demons (see Luke 4:33). Christians have the right to reject all unwanted, unwelcome guests, and they have the right to command them to leave (see Luke 9:1, 10:19). These pests can be evicted by obeying James 4:6-11 properly.

There are exceptions. The man Jesus delivered from the legion of demons in Mark 5:2-15 certainly was possessed. These demons of fear and bondage had completely enslaved the man, causing him to do whatsoever they desired (see Heb. 2:15). Paul referred to this condition in Second Timothy 2:25-26:

> *In meekness instructing those that oppose themselves; if God peradventure will give them repentance to the acknowledging of the truth; and that they may recover themselves out of the snare of the devil, who are taken captive by him at his will* (2 Timothy 2:25-26).

Those who are taken captive by satan at God's will are indeed possessed (see Matt. 18:32-35). It is doubtful that people in that condition could be considered true Christians, although in their deception, they may think they are (see Rom. 8:15).

Frequently, sincere Christians gain liberty from demons by submitting themselves to God. They often obtain deliverance without knowing the full extent of what has been done for them. James 4:7 says, *"Submit yourselves therefore to God. Resist the Devil, and he will flee from you."*

In their warfare against demons, Christians struggle (in their souls) against satan's many enticements and shrewd deceptions. When they cast down ungodly imaginations and logical reasonings, which are contrary to God, they frequently drive out the demonic intruders without realizing it (see 2 Cor. 10:3-5).

Paul taught that it is not people's own thoughts or compulsions that they have to defeat, but sin, which works in their members. To resist an evil thought or impulse is to resist the demon that generates it. Overcoming the sin nature sometimes drives out the wicked spirits that manufacture the works of the flesh (see Rom. 7:20; Gal. 5:19-21).

In the scriptural examples of deliverance, Jesus always dealt with individuals and their attitudes where satanic principalities were implicated. He dealt with the demons themselves where the power, or authority, of satan was involved.

For example, Jesus reprimanded the deaf-mute boy's father and his own disciples, calling them perverse and (therefore) faithless when they could not cure the deaf-mute (see Luke 9:40-41). He then rebuked the unclean spirit of deafness to deliver the boy from his ailment.

Other examples include when Jesus rebuked Peter, calling him satan, because his attitude toward the cross was wrong (see Matt. 16:23). He also reproved the Sadducees for being influenced by the principality of error instead of by the Word and power of God (see Matt. 22:29; 1 John 4:6). Again, when the disciples were fearful in the midst of a storm, they were reproved for having an attitude of dread instead of faith (see Matt. 8:26). He also rebuked the Pharisees for lying (see John 8:44,55).

Although deliverance is the final step in the process of healing, transformation does *not* come through deliverance! *Transformation comes through the renewal of the mind* (see Ps. 51:6-10; Rom. 12:1-2). Renewal without deliverance can leave people in a continual wrestling match in their emotions because the enemy is left within, or in, the walls of their "city." The Scripture says, *"He that hath no rule over his own spirit is like a city that is broken down, and without walls"* (Prov. 25:28; see also Gal. 5:17; Eph. 6:12).

Deliverance without renewal can be dangerous! Jesus said that the unclean spirits *will* return (see Luke 11:24-26). People have to know how to keep their hearts and minds free from satan's evil forces to retain the freedom deliverance brings. By conforming their thoughts and attitudes to God's Word, they can defend their minds and keep themselves free from the return of satan's heinous influence (see Phil. 4:7-9).

And finally, *renewal is a process, not an event.* As a result, true deliverance is also a process (see 2 Cor. 4:16; Phil. 2:12). The fruit of deliverance is peace. It enables people to walk in newness of life as their minds become renewed after the image of God—as it is revealed in Christ (see Col. 3:9-10; 2 Pet. 1:2):

> *Beloved, I wish above all things that thou mayest prosper and be in health, even as thy soul prospereth* (3 John 2).

Chapter 21

TEN STEPS TO VICTORY

I acknowledged my sin to You, and my iniquity I did not hide. I said I will confess my transgressions to the Lord (continually unfolding the past till all is told); then You (instantly) forgave me the guilt and iniquity of my sin.... (Psalm 32:5 AMP).

Repent! Diligent, heartfelt repentance and forgiveness will bring healing obtainable no other way (see Prov. 28:13; John 10:1; 2 Cor. 7:10-11). To obtain mercy, we must show mercy. Jesus warned repeatedly of the necessity of sincere forgiveness of all who have offended or wronged us in any way (see Matt. 18:35).

> *And when ye stand praying, forgive, if ye have ought against any: that your Father also which is in heaven may forgive you your trespasses* (Mark 11:25).

The judgments that people make are turned back upon themselves (see Matt. 7:1-2). If they accuse, they either have done or are doing the very same things they are accusing others of (see Rom. 2:1). If they fail to show mercy and forgive others, they are in violation of the Universal Law of Love and are in sin (see Matt. 6:12-15; Rom. 13:9-10).

When people acknowledge and confess that their resentments (angry reactions to the offenses committed against them), and hurts (which are primarily grief and suppressed anger) are sin, they are forgiven. When people confess their sins and forgive others of their trespasses, they are released and healed from the evil effects and memory of sin (see Prov. 30:12; Heb. 9:14).

The following ten steps performed from the heart with sincere repentance will begin the process of healing that God has promised in His Word (see 2 Chron. 7:14; Ps. 147:3; Luke 4:18).

1. Receive Jesus as Lord

Receive and confess, from your heart, Jesus Christ as your Lord and Savior (see Rom. 10:9-13). Acknowledge Christ as your Judge, Lawgiver, King, and Savior (in accordance with Isaiah 33:22) and as your High Priest (see Rom. 10:9-10; Heb. 4:14).

> For the Lord [Jesus] is our judge, the Lord is our lawgiver, the Lord is our king; He will save us (Isaiah 33:22).

2. Renounce Other Covenants

Identify, confess, and renounce as sin *all* occult involvement and covenants (Ouija boards, Tarot cards, fortune tellers, etc.). Confess and renounce as sin all submission to religious organizations and fraternal lodges (both to the doctrines and government) which limit God or reject the power, presence, or Deity of Jesus (see 2 Cor. 4:2; Tit. 1:16; 1 John 4:2-3). Confess and renounce all harmful soul ties that you have formed with others (see 2 Cor. 6:14).

3. Identify Offenses

Identify and list each *specific* incidence which caused humiliation, hurt, grief, anger, fear, lust, or another offense or trespass that has occurred from each person in your life. Begin with your earliest memories (see the list printed after step ten to remind you of people you are related to or have been involved with).

4. Identify Unclean Spirits

Identify and list the emotional trauma (feelings) that you experienced as a result of each incidence. Examples are: rejection, resentment, hatred, lust, guilt, shame, fear, grief, etc. Identify and list all the unclean spirits that you think you may have received by reason of the above experiences and emotional trauma (step 2-4). For example: rejection, anger, whoredoms (sexual lust), guilt, fear, etc. (*See the Wheel of Nature on page 66 for help in identifying these.*)

5. Acknowledge Your Part

Identify and confess as sin your own part performed in each offense and trespass remembered. Even if your participation was small or incidental, it is still an important part of your healing (see Prov. 28:13). Repent of and confess as sin your own resentment, anger, hate, desire for revenge, grudges, and hurt caused by the above trespasses and sin (see Eph. 4:26; James 5:9).

6. Forgive Audibly

Forgive, as an act of your own will, each *specific* offense and trespass of each *specific* person, by a spoken statement (prayer).

Here is an example of steps four through six:

> *Heavenly Father, in Jesus name I ask you to forgive me of the resentment and hurt that I have held toward my Dad. I freely forgive him for neglecting and rejecting me as a child. I forgive him for the loneliness and fear which I have experienced as a result.*
>
> *I ask you to forgive me of my subsequent rebellion and disobedience. I ask to be forgiven for my anger and all bitter words I have spoken in dishonor of my dad. Heavenly Father, I freely forgive my dad, asking and desiring no recompense or retaliation. I release him from all debt to me. Amen. (See Matthew 6:12-15.)*

Seven Aspects of Forgiveness

Practice each part of forgiveness, considering each offense individually. God said:

"Come now, and let us reason together," saith the Lord: "Though your sins be as scarlet, they shall be as white as snow; though they be red like crimson, they shall be as wool" (Isaiah 1:18).

The seven aspects of forgiveness are abbreviated and listed here for your convenience (see page 175).

- Acknowledge and confess your own participation (*confession*)
- Analyze and confess as sin your negative reaction (*grudge*)
- Forgive the debt (release the desire for *recompense*)
- Justify and pray for your debtors (release the desire for *retaliation*)
- When the offense is ongoing, pray for God to judge the offender (*appeal*)
- Receive God's forgiveness (*faith*)
- Self-forgiveness (freedom from self-hatred, guilt, pride—*healing*)

7. Renounce Unclean Spirits

Once you have completed the process of forgiving all those indebted to you, renounce all spirits listed in step four by name and command them to come out and leave. When possible, this should be done in the presence of and in agreement with a counselor (see Matt. 18:18-19).

8. Have Counselor Renounce Spirits

Have your counselor pray, commanding by name all unclean spirits listed in step four to come out and leave, taking each sin category one at a time. For example: *fear*—bondage, anxiety, confusion (see Luke 4:36).

9. Have Counselor Pray Healing

Have your counselor pray for the healing of a broken heart (see Ps. 147:3), healing of the conscience and consciousness (healing of emotional grief and pain associated with painful memories), and when needed, healing of the physical body (see Heb. 9:14; James 5:14-15).

Also ask your counselor to renounce all guilt and command all soul ties that you have uncovered to be severed by the cross (see Rom. 8:1; 1 John 1:9). Then have the counselor command your personal spirit to be loosed from bondage, awakened, and released (see Luke 4:18). Have the counselor command your spirit to receive spiritual strength and freedom (see Eph. 3:16; Col. 1:11) and command life, light, and peace to come into your heart (see Eph. 5:13-14).

10. Renew Your Mind

Ask your counselor to teach you how to renew your mind (see Rom. 12:1-2). Ask for Scriptures to help you correct old thinking patterns and habits (see Eph. 4:17-32). Ask how to recondition conditioned responses and how to take your thoughts and imaginations captive in obedience to Christ (see 2 Cor. 10:5-6). Here are some examples of Scriptures for rejection: Exodus 21:17; Psalm 22:9-11, 27:10; Mark 11:25-26; Romans 8:28 Ephesians 1:5-6, 6:2; and so forth.

I have *not* included the process or prayers for removing the iniquities of the forefathers in this personal ten-step process. For help with this, see Leviticus 26:39-42 and Daniel 9:2-19.

> *And when ye stand praying, forgive, if ye have ought against any: that your Father also which is in heaven may forgive you your trespasses* (Mark 11:25).

Memory List

1. Grandparents (all, living and dead)

2. Parents (including step or foster parents)

3. Brothers and sisters

4. Other relatives (uncles, aunts, cousins, etc.)

5. School teachers

6. School friends or enemies

7. Boy or girl friends (all, past and present)

8. Husband or wife (including divorced ones)

9. Children and step-children

10. In-laws (include father- and mother-in-law and children's spouses)

11. Employers, employees, co-workers

12. Church pastors, elders, etc.

13. Fellow Christians

14. Neighbors

15. Armed service personnel

16. People in college sororities, fraternities, lodges, clubs, etc.

17. Doctors, mechanics, other professionals, etc.

18. Strangers (and all others not listed)

19. Circumstances (such as trauma caused from negative experiences: fires, auto accidents, sicknesses, operations, etc.)

20. Offenses toward God (God is righteous altogether. All offense toward God should be confessed as a sin.)

And the very God of peace sanctify you wholly; and I pray God your whole spirit and soul and body be preserved blameless unto the coming of our Lord Jesus Christ (1 Thessalonians 5:23).

ADDITIONAL READING

1. Jer. 17:9, John 2:24-25, I Cor. 2:16
2. II Pet. 1:3
3. Hosea 4:6
4. Luke 4:18
5. Rev. 12:9
6. I Cor. 15:55-56
7. The number of eyes vary in different species.
8. I Thes. 3:5; Rev. 12:9-11; I Cor. 10:10
9. James 1:14; Jer. 17:9; Rom. 2:14-15; Rev. 11:18
10. Gal. 5:15
11. Prov. 23:5; Eph. 2:2-3; Acts 14:15
12. Luke 3:8-9
13. I John 3:8
14. John 14:30
15. Luke 4:1-13; Heb. 4:15
16. Rom. 6:11-14
17. Eph. 2:2 John 8:44
18. James 1:13-15
19. Gen. 3:1-6; I Chron. 21:1; John 13:2,27
20. I John 3:4,8,10; Eph. 6:11-12; Matt. 4:1; John 8:44; Acts 13:8-10; I Cor. 7:5; James 4:7
21. Luke 11:15-19
22. John 12:31; Eph. 2:2; II Cor. 4:4
23. John 13:27
24. Acts 5:3
25. Luke 13:11-16
26. Job 2:7
27. Luke 11:17-26
28. Matt. 9:32-33, 12:22, 15:22; John 8:44; Acts 10:38; I Cor. 7:5; I John 3:8
29. Rom. 7:10-11; I Cor. 15:55-56
30. John 13:2; Prov. 21:27
31. John 12:4-6, 13:26-27; Matt. 27:18
32. Gen. 9:16, 17:7; I Sam. 18:3; II Sam. 9:1,6-7; Isa. 55:3; Heb. 13:20; Num. 6:2,5, 30:2-15; Deut. 23:21; Eccl. 5:4-5
33. Deut. 7:2
34. Josh. 9:3-19
35. II Sam. 21:1-10; Eccl. 5:4-6
36. Prov. 5:9-10, 6:26,33; James 4:4

37. Eccl. 7:14

38. Gal. 3:13, 2:18, 5:4;
    I Tim. 5:24-25

39. Hos. 4:6; Num. 15:27-28

40. Deut. 18:9-12

41. II Tim. 1:5; Phil. 3:5; Neh. 9:38,
    10:28-29

42. II Tim. 3:5; Psalm 78:40-41;
    Heb. 11:6

43. Acts 1:8

44. II Tim. 4:2-4; Matt. 22:29-32

45. Mark 7:13; Matt. 13:58

46. Acts 9:1-2; I Tim. 4:1

47. II Tim. 3:5; II Cor. 4:2, 11:3-4;
    Eccl. 5:4-6

48. Prov. 5:22, 28:13

49. Eph. 6:4

50. Rom. 7:18-19

51. Heb. 2:6-7

52. Eph. 6:12

53. I Cor. 9:26

54. I Tim. 1:18, 2:1-2

55. II Chron. 18:30

56. Dan. 10:12-13

57. Dan. 6:7-13

58. Lev. 26:39-42; Luke 3:7-14;
    Jonah 3:4-10

59. Matt. 6:23

60. Psalm 9:17; Rom. 1:32; Gen.
    15:16, 19:9,13-15

61. II Thes. 3:1-2; Prov. 29:2

62. Exod. 17:8-14

63. II Chron. 29:1-10, 30:4-20, 31:1,
    33:1-10-17

64. Matt. 7:18

65. **Twelve Universal Laws of the
    Universe**

    Praise and Worship:
    Matt. 6:21-24; Luke 11:41;

    Psalms 66:18, 22:3, 16:11, 50:23

    Hearing, Judging whether to
    Accept or Reject (thus Obey or
    Disobey) that which is heard:
    John 5:30; Luke 8:18; Isa.
    1:19-20

    Dominion, Voluntary and
    Involuntary Submission:
    Psalms 94:20

    John 8:34-36; Rom. 6:16; II Pet.
    2:19

    Stewardship, Responsibility, and
    Faithfulness: Luke 12:48, I
    Cor. 4:2; Luke 16:10-12; Luke
    19:13-27

    Promotion and Demotion: Psalm
    75:6-7; Matt. 23:12; Mark
    9:35;

    Prov. 3:34-35, 18:12, 22:4

    Patience and Persistence,
    Importunity: Luke 11:5-10,
    18:1-8, 21:19; Heb. 6:12

    Division and Unity: Matt. 12:25,
    18:18-20; James 1:6-8; Gen.
    11:1-8

    Sowing and Reaping, Harvest:
    Gal. 6:7-8; Gen. 1:11-12;
    Matt. 7:1-2,17-18; Luke 6:38;
    II Cor. 9:6; Isa. 3:10-11;
    Prov. 24:11-12

Sin and Death: Rom. 7:21-23; Ezek. 18:20; Gen. 2:17

Righteousness, The Royal Law, or The Law of Love: Lev. 18:5;

Deut. 6:25; Rom. 13:8-10, 9:30-31, 10:4; Gal. 5:14; James 2:8

Faith and Action, Works: Rom. 1:17, 3:27; Matt. 9:29, 17:20;

Mark 9:23, 11:23-24; James 2:20-24

The Spirit of Life and Liberty: Rom. 8:1-4; John 8:35-36;

James 1:25, 2:12-13; Rom. 4:6-8; Gal. 5:1,13

66. Luke 3:9

67. Josh. 6:18-19, 7:20-25

68. II Sam. 13:6-16; Deut. 22:25-26

69. I Sam. 15:2-3, 17-30

70. II Sam. 11:1-25, 12:9

71. James 1:13

72. I Cor. 13:12; James 1:23-25

73. John 1:14

74. Eph. 5:8

75. Exod. 19:10-24; Heb. 12:18-21, 4:15-16

76. II Tim. 2:20-21; Rom. 9:21-23; II Cor. 5:19

77. II Cor. 4:7

78. I Kings 7:45-47; I Cor. 15:45-49

79. Gen. 1:26-27

80. John 16:7; Acts 2:17

81. Eph. 5:22-32; Heb. 3:6; II Tim. 2:20-21

82. I Cor. 3:9,16-17

83. Gen. 2:23-24; I Cor. 11:3; Gal. 2:20

84. II Pet. 1:4; Acts 5:32

85. I Pet. 3:7; Gen. 3:1-6

86. Isa. 14:12-14

87. Jude 1:6

88. Acts 13:10-11

89. I Cor. 6:17,19; Ezek. 36:26-27

90. Rom. 7:17-18

91. Gen. 3:14

92. John 3:19-20; Eph. 5:8-13

93. Mark 14:38; Matt. 26:41; Rom. 1:9

94. Matt. 18:2-4

95. Heb. 3:12-13

96. Rom. 12:2; Psalm 51:10

97. Rom. 3:23; Heb. 3:6-12; Psalm 51:5

98. Jer. 18:1-4

99. Eph. 2:10

100. John 8:44

101. Rom. 9:20-22; Acts 5:1-5

102. Eph. 2:3

103. Luke 16:15

104. Rom. 8:6-7

105. Prov. 4:23

106. I Tim. 2:14

107. II Cor. 4:4; Gen. 1:26-28

108. Exod. 7:1; John 10:34-35

109. Rom. 6:16

110. Isa. 14:13-14

111. Psalm 51:5; Eph. 2:2
112. Rom. 7:23
113. Psalms 95:8-10; Dan. 5:20; Rom. 3:9-10
114. James 1:14-15
115. II Cor. 11:3-4; Eph. 4:22
116. Job 19:26
117. Heb. 1:10-12
118. II Cor. 5:1; I Cor. 15:44-50
119. Gen. 2:7
120. Gen. 46:26; Exod. 1:5; Ezek. 18:20
121. Luke 10:21
122. Rom. 1:32; I Cor. 13:6
123. Mark 1:41; Acts 7:54
124. See: *Rightly Dividing the Word* Ira L. Milligan, Servant Ministries, Inc., 2000 (pages 83-87)
125. Matt. 26:41
126. John 1:13
127. Rev. 22:17
128. I Sam. 16:7; Heb. 4:12
129. Rom. 8:7
130. Eph. 2:3
131. Heb. 4:12
132. Eph. 1:11
133. Rom. 7:1,7-9,19-25
134. Rom. 1:9
135. Eph. 2:2-3
136. Isa. 1:19-20; Rev. 22:17
137. Gal. 5:16
138. Heb. 5:14
139. Gen. 2:9
140. I Cor. 7:32-33; Gal. 1:10
141. I Cor. 15:33, 7:29,32-34
142. II Cor. 11:3
143. Gen. 3:8, 6:3; I John 3:9
144. II Tim. 4:10
145. II Tim. 1:5
146. Heb. 7:9-10; Acts 17:28
147. Rom. 2:14-15
148. Heb. 5:14, Isa. 7:16
149. Heb. 12:15
150. Eph. 4:23; Rom. 2:15, 7:25, 8:5-7
151. Rom. 6:14, 8:13; II Cor. 10:5; Matt. 12:37
152. Rom. 7:5
153. Matt. 12:33
154. Col. 3:2-4; Rom. 6:16-19
155. Isa. 55:7-9; Prov. 16:3
156. Luke 16:15
157. Phil. 3:7-8
158. Matt. 6:21; See: The Law of Worship,
159. Heb. 3:8-10; Rom. 7:18-19
160. Gen. 3:17
161. Acts 5:32
162. Rom. 16:19-20; Phil. 1:9-10
163. I John 3:7,10, 2:15
164. John 16:8-11; Rev. 12:10-11; Matt. 23:23
165. I John 5:4; Heb. 11:1
166. John 8:31-32

167. Eph. 6:12; Col. 2:13-15; Psalms 94:20
168. Gen. 3:4-5
169. Prov. 25:28; II Tim. 2:26; II Cor. 11:3-4
170. Gal. 5:17; Rom. 8:7
171. James 3:15-16
172. Rom. 7:23
173. Prov. 5:22
174. II Tim. 2:25-26
175. Luke 9:54-55
176. II Tim. 3:13
177. Eph. 1:21
178. Acts 19:13; Matt. 12:45; I Tim. 4:1
179. Luke 9:42; Mark 9:17,25
180. Isa. 61:3
181. I Sam. 20:30-31,34
182. Luke 11:24-26
183. Hos. 5:4
184. Matt. 7:18-20
185. Matt. 13:24-25,39; Luke 3:7-9
186. I John 3:8; Matt. 7:15-17
187. Gen. 4:5-8; II Sam. 3:27, 11:14-17; Acts 7:54-59; I John 3:15
188. II Cor. 2:11
189. John 8:32; Isa. 55:7; Acts 2:40
190. Acts 5:3
191. Rom. 8:5-7
192. Prov. 28:13; II Cor. 4:2
193. Gen. 22:17; Exod. 23:22,27; Luke 10:19

194. Gen. 2:7; III John 2; Heb. 4:12
195. I Thes. 5:23
196. Tit. 1:15
197. Gen. 10:9-10
198. Eccl. 10:19
199. I Tim. 6:7-10
200. III John 1:9-10
201. Isa. 14:12-15
202. John 6:15; Phil. 2:7-8
203. Matt. 26:41; Mark 14:38; Rom. 1:9, 7:16-20
204. John 1:13; I Pet. 4:3; II Pet. 1:21; Rev. 22:17
205. Isa. 46:10
206. Eph. 1:11; Matt. 12:18
207. **Which is the Spirit of God:** John 14:10, 20:28; II Cor. 5:19; I Tim. 3:16
208. Luke 4:1-13; Matt. 26:38-39; Phil. 2:3-8; Heb. 4:15
209. James 4:17; Acts 24:16
210. Heb. 9:14
211. Gen. 3:2-3
212. **The Law of Righteousness (Love)** Rom. 2:14-15, 13:9-10; Gal. 5:14
213. Rom. 2:14-15; Matt. 18:3-4
214. Rom. 8:2; John 8:34-36
215. Matt. 8:26, 14:31, 16:8, 17:17
216. I Pet. 3:21; Heb. 11:1
217. Rom. 9:1
218. I John 3:21

219. I Sam. 24:4-5; II Sam. 24:10

220. John 8:7-9; I Cor. 11:31-32

221. Psalms 1:1; John 13:2

222. John 6:63; Luke 4:2-14

223. Gen. 6:3

224. John 16:8-13; Rom. 7:18,23

225. John 8:31-32

226. Prov. 4:23

227. Heb. 4:12

228. Jer. 17:9; Eph. 4:18; Heb. 3:10-15

229. Matt. 5:8; Luke 8:15

230. Isa. 14:12-14

231. Psalms 94:20; Rom. 6:16

232. Eph. 4:23

233. II Cor. 4:4; Prov. 16:2; James 1:14-15

234. John 10:10

235. I Thes. 3:5; I John 2:16; James 1:14

236. Rev. 12:9; II Cor. 10:5

237. Matt. 12:37

238. Rev. 12:10-11; Luke 16:14-15; Rom. 2:1

239. I Cor. 10:10; Psalms 94:20; Rom. 7:5,8-11; Ezek. 33:11

240. I Cor. 1:18

241. John 10:1

242. I John 5:3

243. Luke 9:51

244. Eph. 1:5-6

245. Psalms 16:11

246. Mark 8:34; Col. 3:1-5

247. Gen. 1:27-31

248. Col. 3:2

249. Luke 14:26-27,33

250. Eph. 5:24-32

251. Gen. 2:8-9; Heb. 12:2

252. Phil. 1:29; Acts 5:40-41

253. Matt. 15:8-9

254. I Pet. 4:12-14; Heb. 10:34; II Cor. 4:16-18

255. II Tim. 2:12

256. Col. 1:24

257. Rom. 7:5

258. I Tim. 6:9-10; Col. 3:5

259. I Tim. 6:9

260. Gen. 2:9, 3:1-6

261. Gen. 4:1

262. Phil. 3:8

263. Rom. 7:18

264. Jdgs. 16:19

265. Eph. 2:2-3; James 1:14-15

266. Prov. 27:20; Eccl. 8:1; John 4:13

267. Jude 1:7

268. John 17:3

269. I John 2:16

270. I Cor. 15:47-48; Rom. 8:20

271. James 1:14-15

272. Tit. 1:15

273. Prov. 4:7

274. Prov. 8:12, 15:2,7

275. I Cor. 2:13

276. Matt. 6:33

277. John 4:13-14
278. Psalms 42:7
279. John 1:14, 6:51; I Cor. 10:3-4
280. Rom. 7:5
281. Acts 17:21
282. I John 2:15-18; I Cor. 3:16
283. Col. 3:5
284. I Cor. 8:1
285. II Thes. 2:3-4
286. I John 2:18
287. I Cor. 1:18
288. II Cor. 12:10
289. I Cor. 15:43
290. Phil. 3:19
291. Acts 12:21-23; John 7:18
292. Luke 18:10-14; James 4:5-6
293. Col. 3:5; I Cor. 6:9-10
294. Col. 3:2
295. Matt. 6:33; Psalms 37:4
296. Phil. 4:11
297. Psalms 119:165; Rom. 8:38-39; Matt. 11:6
298. Gen. 31:30-36
299. I Tim. 6:9-10
300. I Tim. 6:7
301. Col. 3:2
302. I Cor. 7:29-31
303. Psalms 62:10
304. Prov. 23:5
305. Mark 10:21-23; Prov. 13:12
306. Job 1:21
307. Phil. 3:7-14; Luke 16:11
308. Col. 2:2-3; Luke 10:42
309. Eph. 4:28
310. I John 4:5-6
311. Matt. 6:24
312. I John 2:15-18
313. I Tim. 6:9-10
314. Isa. 61:3
315. Luke 16:13; Mark 10:21-22; Prov. 13:12
316. I Tim. 3:1-3, 4:1-2; Eph. 4:19
317. Rom. 2:1
318. Gen. 3:12
319. Col. 3:5-6; Rom. 1:18
320. Heb. 3:11-13
321. Eph. 2:12; Gen. 3:23-24; Prov. 13:12
322. I Cor. 10:14
323. Acts 15:29
324. John 4:13-14; Prov. 2:3-5
325. Isa. 52:3, 50:1
326. James 4:4
327. Jdgs. 11:1-3
328. Jdgs. 11:6-11
329. Jdgs. 11:30-31,34-39
330. Hos. 2:2-5; John 4:16-18
331. Jdgs. 13:2-3, 14:1-3
332. Jdgs. 15:1-8, 16:1-3,28
333. Col. 2:20-23
334. Acts 17:22
335. Matt. 5:32

336. Gen. 2:22-25; Mark 10:6-9

337. Gen. 2:22-24, 3:16

338. Eph. 5:33, Amplified

339. I Cor. 7:2-5; Gen. 24:67

340. Heb. 13:4

341. Acts 24:16

342. I Cor. 8:12

343. Rom. 13:1

344. Heb. 13:4

345. Gen. 3:16; I Cor. 11:3

346. Rom. 1:21-28

347. II Pet. 2:19

348. I Cor. 15:34; I John 3:9

349. Jdgs. 16:19

350. Rom. 11:8

351. Hos. 5:4

352. Matt. 5:27-28

353. John 8:34

354. Rom. 6:16

355. Luke 21:34; Prov. 30:20

356. Gen. 3:8; Isa. 59:1-2

357. Acts 2:37-38, 15:9; Heb. 9:14

358. II Cor. 7:9-11

359. Jer. 18:12

360. Acts 13:10; I Cor. 7:2-5; Rom. 7:19-21

361. Heb. 9:14

362. Eph. 1:5-6

363. Gen. 1:27; Rom. 8:29; II Cor. 3:18

364. Psalms 147:3; Psalms 27:10

365. Heb. 9:14; I John 1:9, 3:21

366. Rom. 14:23

367. Rom. 8:24-25; Matt. 8:26

368. Heb. 2:14-15

369. I John 3:20

370. Rom. 6:23

371. I Pet. 3:10; Gal. 2:20

372. John 17:3

373. John 10:10; Luke 14:33

374. Gen. 3:10

375. Prov. 28:1

376. Col. 3:14

377. I Cor. 7:15

378. Luke 12:15,34

379. Prov. 22:13

380. Jdgs. 6:11-15

381. Prov. 7:10-11

382. Prov. 26:16; I Sam. 21:12-15

383. Ezra 4:23

384. Eph. 4:27

385. *Fears and Phobias,* Dr. Tony Whitehead, Arco Publishing, Inc., 1983

386. Psalms 44:14-16; James 3:16

387. Luke 8:26-39

388. Mark 5:2-5

389. Deut. 32:30-36; Luke 11:26

390. Mark 5:13

391. I John 4:18

392. Luke 8:37

393. Luke 11:24-26

394. Prov. 9:10; I John 5:3
395. Josh. 9:11-27, 10:3-8; Psalms 94:22-23
396. See Note 37, Page 20
397. Acts 5:32
398. II Tim. 1:7
399. Phil. 1:21
400. II Cor. 3:17
401. Luke 10:19
402. I John 4:18
403. I John 5:3, 3:21-22
404. I Cor. 2:16
405. I Cor. 3:21-23; Rom. 8:28
406. Phil. 1:28
407. Rom. 8:31
408. Isa. 14:12-15
409. Luke 8:27-29
410. John 8:43-44
411. Rom. 10:17
412. II Tim. 3:4; Rev. 4:11
413. Gal. 1:10
414. John 5:44
415. Acts 8:5-23
416. Acts 8:20; Rom. 8:5-6
417. John 12:26
418. Matt. 13:57
419. Gal. 1:10
420. Isa. 19:14
421. I Cor. 2:10
422. I Cor. 11:1
423. II Tim. 4:3; Matt. 15:12-14

424. I Cor. 4:3
425. Matt. 17:20
426. Luke 9:45; Matt. 16:23
427. Luke 9:46-48
428. Prov. 26:16, 12:24; Phil. 2:12; Rom. 12:1-2
429. Prov. 21:25-26, 18:9, 26:16
430. Lev. 26:39-42
431. Exod. 34:7
432. II Cor. 10:5-6
433. Phil. 2:7
434. John 5:41
435. Matt. 17:21
436. Neh. 1:3-7; Dan. 9:3-24; Isa. 58:6-12
437. Lev. 26:39-42
438. Mark 9:24-29
439. Mark 9:21-23
440. Acts 5:7-10
441. James 1:22-26
442. Luke 12:1-3
443. John 5:41
444. Acts 16:16-18; I Sam. 28:7
445. I Kings 22:10-12,19-24
446. I Kings 22:24
447. I Tim. 4:1
448. Acts 21:10-11
449. Isa. 20:2-4; Ezek. 4:1-17, 5:1-4
450. I Cor. 14:29
451. John 16:13-15
452. II Tim. 3:13

453. Gen. 3:1-5; John 8:44; Isa. 14:12-14

454. Gen. 3:14; Jude 1:6; James 3:15

455. II Tim. 2:25-26

456. Acts 2:21,38

457. I John 3:8

458. II Pet. 2:4

459. I John 2:1

460. I John 4:10; Heb. 7:25

461. I John 3:2

462. Tit. 3:2

463. Rev. 12:7; James 3:9-10

464. Prov. 11:9

465. Acts 14:15; James 5:17

466. Prov. 10:18

467. John 9:41

468. Prov. 11:12

469. Prov. 14:1,21; Eph. 5:22,33

470. Rom. 13:9-10

471. I Cor. 10:32

472. John 8:3-11

473. II Cor. 10:6

474. II Thes. 3:14-15

475. Prov. 11:12

476. Deut. 29:19-20; Acts 5:1-5

477. Prov. 11:12, 12:15

478. Luke 22:28; Heb. 4:15

479. Eph. 6:12

480. Matt. 12:36-37

481. Rom. 2:14-15

482. Prov. 16:18; Matt. 12:22; II Cor. 4:4

483. I Cor. 3:3-6

484. Matt. 16:16-18; I John 1:6-7, 3:14, 4:20-21

485. John 16:2

486. Eph. 4:3,13

487. Eph. 1:16-18

488. Job 42:10; III John 14

489. Matt. 7:1-2; Rom. 1:18, 2:1-5; Prov. 19:19; II Sam. 12:5-12

490. James 1:20

491. John 6:70

492. John 15:3

493. Matt. 16:23

494. Phil. 1:15-18

495. Gen. 13:2-9; I Cor. 7:30-31

496. Prov. 26:20-21, 28:25

497. Prov. 12:13

498. Prov. 27:4

499. II Pet. 1:9

500. Matt. 12:7

501. Rev. 1:19, 4:1

502. Matt. 11:12, 16:18

503. Prov. 22:10

504. I John 3:15

505. Gen. 3:12, 4:3-8

506. Gen. 13:2,5-9, 14:8-16, 21:9-12,25

507. Acts 15:1-2,5-20,36-40

508. Matt. 18:7

509. Eccl. 4:1

510. Rom. 8:28

511. II Cor. 9:12-13

512. I Cor. 1:18

513. Psalms 51:1-10; Heb. 9:14

514. James 3:15; 4:7-8

515. James 4:1-12

516. Prov. 26:28; Matt. 26:59-62, 27:18

517. Mark 11:25

518. Matt. 5:38-41

519. Matt. 5:44; Acts 3:26

520. Hos. 10:12

521. Acts 7:9, 13:44-45, 17:5

522. Matt. 5:27-28; Rom. 2:1-6

523. Psalms 41:9; John 13:1,18

524. Lev. 19:17-18

525. Mark 15:10

526. Mark 2:18; John 7:12, 9:16,24, 12:19

527. Num. 5:14

528. Luke 15:27-28

529. Ezek. 25:15

530. Prov. 6:34

531. Jer. 18:18; John 8:44

532. I John 3:12-15; Mal. 2:10; Matt. 5:21-24, 6:15; Mark 11:25-26

533. James 5:9; Lev. 19:17-18

534. Matt. 6:15, 18:34-35

535. I John 3:11-12

536. Rom. 13:1-2

537. I Cor. 11:3

538. Acts 24:16

539. I Cor. 11:3; Eph. 5:22, 6:1-6

540. Heb. 13:17

541. I Cor. 7:13-16

542. I Tim. 5:8

543. I Pet. 3:1; I Cor. 14:34

544. Rom. 16:1-6; I Tim. 2:12; Rev. 2:20; Heb. 13:17

545. Jer. 18:18

546. Ezra 4:18-23; Neh. 6:7-13

547. Gal. 2:4, 3:1

548. Jdgs. 16:5,15-17

549. II Sam. 13:3-15

550. I Cor. 7:2-5

551. Jdgs. 14:17

552. Acts 8:9-11,18-23; I Sam. 12:3

553. Prov. 20:1, 23:29-35; Isa. 28:7

554. Matt. 26:41

555. Lev. 26:15-16; Lam. 5:17

556. Exod. 15:26; Num. 12:1-15; II Chron. 16:10-12, 21:12-19, 26:16-21

557. Luke 13:11-13,16

558. Rom. 11:9-10

559. II Kings 13:14; I Tim. 5:23

560. Gen. 27:1

561. Matt. 12:22; John 9:1-3; Acts 10:38; II Tim. 2:15

562. Psalms 37:7; Luke 21:19; Heb. 10:36, 12:1

563. Eccl. 7:9

564. Isa. 8:19-22

565. Exod. 15:24, 16:2, 17:3; Deut. 1:27, 28:47-48

566. Acts 8:9-11,18, 13:6-8

567. I Cor. 12:25-27

568. Col. 3:5

569. Luke 11:24-26

570. Prov. 14:9; Num. 33:55; Josh. 23:5-13; John 8:34

571. I Kings 19:1-3

572. Rev. 2:20

573. Esth. 1:15-22

574. Rom. 13:1

575. Acts 23:5; II Pet. 2:10; Exod. 16:8

576. I Tim. 5:17; I Pet. 5:2-3; Acts 15:6,22-23

577. Rom. 13:1; Eph. 5:25, 6:4,9

578. I Sam. 16:5,11

579. I Sam. 17:17-18,28-32

580. Rom. 8:28; Gen. 50:20

581. II Sam. 10:1-4

582. Eccl. 7:26; Heb. 12:13-16

583. Prov. 7:25-27

584. II Sam. 11:1-27

585. I Sam. 18:11, 24:11-12; II Sam. 11:22-25

586. II Sam. 12:1-14; Matt. 12:37

587. Prov. 17:13, Isa. 40:2

588. Prov. 6:32-33

589. Ezek. 18:20; Gen. 2:17

590. Rom. 6:23; I Cor. 15:55-56; James 1:15

591. II Tim. 1:10; Psalms 103:10-12; Gen. 8:22

592. Prov. 18:20-21; Jer. 6:19, 17:10; Isa. 3:10

593. Acts 26:9-11; II Cor. 11:23-25

594. Gen. 25:31-33, 27:18-24,35-36; Heb. 12:16-17

595. Gen. 37:3,27-35, 47:8-9; Acts 7:9

596. Gen. 47:18-27; Exod. 1:9-11

597. Exod. 12:5-11

598. Num. 32:23

599. Psalms 119:89

600. Rom. 7:5; Gal. 5:19-21

601. I Kings 20:1,23-25

602. Gen. 3:1-5

603. Gen. 3:4-5

604. Eph. 2:3; I Cor. 6:18; Matt. 12:36-37

605. Eph. 6:12

606. Rom 1:21

607. II Cor. 10:3-4

608. Deut. 21:20; Luke 21:34; Prov. 20:1, 31:6-7

609. John 12:4-6, 13:2; Matt. 27:18

610. II Cor. 2:11; John 8:34

611. I Cor. 6:20; John 8:31-36

612. James 1:25

613. Matt. 11:12; Luke 4:18, 17:20-21; Gal. 5:17

614. Jdgs. 2:1-15; Deut. 28:13-15, 43-44

615. Jdgs. 2:16, 3:15, 4:3-7

616. Rom. 5:12-14

617. Psalms 103:2-3

618. Exod. 15:25-26; Isa. 53:4-5

619. I John 1:9; Psalms 103:3
620. Tit. 1:15, Heb. 12:15
621. Acts 15:9; Heb. 9:14; Rom. 8:1
622. Rom. 6:4
623. John 11:25
624. Rom. 5:17; I Pet. 4:10-11
625. Rom. 8:11
626. Eph. 2:1
627. Rev. 3:1; II Cor. 1:19-20; Eph. 3:20, 5:14
628. Rom. 6:19; Col. 1:20-21
629. Matt. 12:28-29
630. Acts 19:13-16
631. Luke 11:22
632. Prov. 26:2; Psalms 94:20
633. Prov. 28:13; Lev. 26:39-42
634. Rom. 6:16; II Pet. 2:19
635. Prov. 5:22; Eph. 4:8
636. Matt. 18:18-19; Luke 4:33-35
637. Luke 11:24-26; Mark 9:17-24-25
638. Luke 8:35
639. Eph. 6:12
640. Eph. 6:11-12; Rom. 6:16,19
641. I Cor. 6:17; Rom. 1:9
642. Luke 4:33
643. Luke 9:1, 10:19
644. Heb. 2:15
645. Matt. 18:32-35
646. Rom. 8:15
647. II Cor. 10:3-5
648. Rom. 7:20; Gal. 5:19-21

649. Luke 9:40-41
650. Matt. 16:23
651. Matt. 22:29; I John 4:6
652. Matt. 8:26
653. John 8:44,55
654. Rom. 12:1-2; Psalms 51:6-10
655. Eph. 6:12; Gal. 5:17; Prov. 25:28
656. Luke 11:24-26
657. Phil. 4:7-9
658. II Cor. 4:16; Phil. 2:12
659. II Pet. 1:2; Col. 3:9-10
660. Prov. 28:13; John 10:1; II Cor. 7:10-11
661. Matt. 18:35
662. Matt. 7:1-2
663. Rom. 2:1
664. Rom. 13:9-10; Matt. 6:12-15
665. Prov. 30:12; Heb. 9:14
666. II Chron. 7:14; Psalms 147:3; Luke 4:18
667. Rom. 10:9-13
668. II Cor. 4:2; Tit. 1:16; I John 4:2-3
669. II Cor. 6:14
670. Prov. 28:13
671. Eph. 4:26; James 5:9
672. Matt. 6:12-15
673. Matt. 18:18-19
674. Luke 4:36
675. Psalms 147:3
676. Heb. 9:14; James 5:14-15
677. Rom. 8:1; I John 1:9

678. Luke 4:18
679. Eph. 3:16; Col. 1:11
680. Eph. 5:13-14
681. Rom. 12:1-2
682. Eph. 4:17-32
683. II Cor. 10:5-6

BIBLIOGRAPHY

Milligan, Ira L., *Rightly Dividing the Word* (Tioga, LA: Servant Ministries, Inc., 2000).

Sandford, John and Paula, *Healing the Wounded Spirit* (South Plainfield, N.J. : Bridge Publishing, Inc., 1985).

Young's Literal Translation of the Holy Bible, ed. Robert Young (Grand Rapids, MI: Baker Book House, 1898).

Whitehead, Dr. Tony, *Fears and Phobias* (New York, N.Y. : Arco Publishing, Inc., 1983).

ABOUT THE AUTHOR

Ira has served God since 1962. In 1986 Ira and his wife Judy founded Servant Ministries Inc. They travel and present seminars such as: *Dreams and Their Interpretation; Counseling and Inner Healing; Spiritual Warfare;* and *Prophets and Personal Prophecy.*

Ira Milligan has taught classes on counseling as a guest lecturer at Oral Roberts University. He presently lives in Tioga, Louisiana.

Ira and his wife have raised four children and have ten grandchildren.

For information about seminars conducted in your church, write or e-mail:

Address:

Servant Ministries Inc.
PO Box 1120
Tioga, LA 71477

E-mail:

servantministries@suddenlink.net

BOOKS BY IRA MILLIGAN

Understanding the Dreams You Dream (Revised)
Biblical Keys for Hearing God's Voice in the Night

Understanding the Dreams You Dream, Vol. II
Every Dreamer's Handbook

The Hidden Power of Covenant
Releasing the Fullness of the Blessing of the Gospel

Hidden Mysteries of the Bible, Vol. I
52 Lesson Foundational Bible Study Course

Hidden Mysteries of the Bible, Vol. II
52 Lesson Advanced Bible Study Course

Rightly Dividing the Word
A Comprehensive Guide to the Scriptures

Truth or Consequences
The Truth Will Make You Free

The Master's Voice
A Guide to Personal Ministry

Euroclydon
Illustrating the Four Winds

The Scorpion Within
Revealing the Eight Demonic Roots of Sin

Additional copies of this book and other
book titles from DESTINY IMAGE are
available at your local bookstore.

Call toll-free: 1-800-722-6774.

Send a request for a catalog to:

Destiny Image® Publishers, Inc.

P.O. Box 310
Shippensburg, PA 17257-0310

*"Speaking to the Purposes of God for This
Generation and for the Generations to Come."*

**For a complete list of our titles,
visit us at www.destinyimage.com.**